Saltwater Seasons

Saltwater Seasons

Recollections of a Country Woman

by Esther Wood

ISBN—0-89272-108-1
Library of Congress Catalog Card Number: 80-69562

Down East Books, Camden, Maine

Printed in the United States of America

for Emily

Contents

The Home Place

The Village

Country Ways

Country Foods

Saltwater Seasons

Preface

At my home place the bay marks the coming and the going of the seasons.

In November the coves have skim ice on their margins. In the cold winters the bay is ice-sealed by February. In March the ice breaks up and in April it goes out leaving the bay blue and placid. The appearance of the bay changes with the seasons. In the winter it is white. In the spring and the summer it may be shrouded with fog or hidden by showers or bright under the sun. In the fall it has its gray days and its blue days; when the line gale comes, it has its black days.

The seasons bring changes in country living. Each season has its own chores. Winter has fire tending and snow shoveling. Spring has housecleaning and planting. Summer has gardening and berrying. Fall has bulb planting and readying the house and yard for cold weather. Each season has its own pleasures. Winter has long evenings for reading. In the summer there is the entertaining of visitors. In the fall there is time for walking.

Country people change their foods with the seasons. In the winter we eat the old favorites of our forebears—hash and chowders and baked beans. In the spring we have rhubarb and dandelion greens. In the summer we eat vegetables, green from the garden, and berries straight from the patch, and fish fresh from the bay. In the fall we have native apples and cider.

Country living is always interesting, always changing. It follows the pattern of the shifting seasons.

Some of these pieces have been published in magazines and newspapers. I am grateful for permission to include them in this collection. I particularly wish to thank the *Ellsworth American* for giving permission to reprint several pieces which have appeared in my weekly column.

It is appropriate to dedicate my recollections to Emily Candage Ellis. She and I have shared many seasons—all of them saltwater.

The Home Place

Mother always called her eastern kitchen window "my sunny window."

Perhaps that was why I referred to my bedroom window as "my rainy window."

Both windows were well named. The kitchen window caught the first glow of the rising sun and was filled with sunshine all the forenoons of pleasant days. In summer Mother sat beside it while she picked over berries or shelled peas; in fall the sills held jars of apple jelly; in winter geraniums sunned themselves there, and in the spring a stand was moved in front of the window where boxes of slender seedlings were coaxed to sturdy growth.

The nine-paned window of my under-the-eaves bedroom faced east, where it caught the full force of the easterly rainstorms. On stormy nights I used to lie awake and listen to the drops as they hit the window. As a result I became an expert in the sound of rain. A summer storm sent gusts of water against the panes almost as though a man in the cloud had turned on a faucet. The fall gales that combined wind and rain shook my window and pelted it with rain. Winter storms had icy fingers that knocked sharply on the glass. Spring showers were so gentle that I had to listen carefully in order to hear the soft tap of the drops.

Not only could I hear the rain against the panes, I could also hear the water as it drained off the ell roof to the flat shed roof below. Sometimes the fast flow of the water made me think of a waterfall; sometimes the slow dripping seemed to say, "Go to sleep, sleep, sleep." And it always seemed that I did go to sleep more quickly when I heard rain against the panes and water on the roof.

On pleasant nights Mother left the curtain at my window raised so that I could see the stars in the eastern sky. I liked to select the brightest star and greet it with the wishful salutation,

> Star bright, star light
> First star I've seen tonight,
> Wish I may, wish I might,
> Have the wish I wish tonight.

When Mother got up in the morning she drew the shade at my window lest the rising sun wake me too early. When I did awaken, I often saw birds silhouetted against the shade. Phone wires stretched from a pole near the well curb to the corner of the shed within a few feet of my window. There the birds loved to perch. In the winter the chickadees swung there. In early summer a robin stayed on the wire while he guarded his mate nesting in the backyard lilac. But it was in late August that I had the best show. Then the barn swallows brought their fledglings to the wire for an early morning trial of their wings. Their twittering always waked me to watch the darting flight of the old birds and the hesitant flying of the young ones.

The tapping of the rain, the splashing of water and the sound of the songbirds were not the only sounds I heard as I lay in my bed. On April nights I was lulled to sleep by the peepers in the bog by the brook. Their piping was sharp and high pitched, very different from the liquid call of the thrush and the lonely cry of the loons that I heard on summer twilights. In the fall I listened for the honking of the geese winging south for the winter. Winter nights were usually silent save for the occasional bark of a fox and the merry jingling of bells on a passing sleigh.

Father used to tell me that when he was a very small child he was startled from sleep by the hoot of an owl on a pine tree near the nursery window. Mother liked to recall that in her childhood the whip-poor-wills filled the summer air with their "whipping." But I heard neither poor-wills nor owls. Likely Model T's had driven them from Friend's Corner by the time of my childhood.

Father, too, had a favorite window. It had no name. It was the kitchen window that faced the south with a view of the pasture, the Bay, the Neck, and the Sand Point. He staked his claim to the window by laying down an edict that Mother always observed, "This window is to have no white curtain. When I stand in front of it, I want to see the view. Windows are for looking."

the old barn

Our Friend's Corner barn has changed little in more than half a century. Indeed, I think that Great-uncle Otis, who never returned from the Civil War, would recognize the interior of the old structure. I am sure that my Grandfather Maddocks would feel very much at home there though he would regret the passing of the cow and the horse, and would marvel at the car and power lawnmower.

Grandfather would recognize in the barn many of his tools, the scythe, the sickle, the sheep shears, the wheelbarrow, and the cider press. I'm sure that he would be glad his tools are still in use, though he would grit his teeth at the sight of the nicks in the scythe blade and deplore the press becoming a catchall for odds and ends.

The barn holds relics of my paternal grandfather's years before the mast: his compass in its stained binnacle, his ship's bell, several remnants of patched sails, and numerous firkins. But I treasure most his dough-table, a fit heirloom from a captain-grandfather who started his seafaring career in the cooking galley. The pine table with two drawers has a protecting rim around three sides of the top lest a pitch of the schooner jar the pots and pans from the table.

My father and his brother failed to follow in the nautical footsteps of their father. Indeed, by their childhood the day of the wooden sailing craft had passed. Their hometown became a booming granite village, with cutting at the "Pittsburg", "Chase's", "White's", and the "Doorstone." It was natural for them to become stonecutters. In the barn are their "kits"—heavy wooden boxes filled with drills and hammers.

I make no pretense of using the stonecutters' tools, but other possessions of my father and my uncle I do use. Father's grain bins are filled with treasures and have their tops nailed down. Uncle's bins hold garden stakes and peat moss. One tool chest holds worn carpenter's tools. The second one holds the better tools and is kept locked because I am a misplacer of tools. I use the old hammer, the saws and the screwdriver with great gusto and no skill.

The shelves along the east side of the barn give the old barn a literary flavor. They hold several hundred books. Some are faded novels of the era of Harold Bell Wright; others are sample textbooks from the years when Father was the supervisor of schools. Many are religious books and bear on their title page the name of Reverend Ebenezar Bean, a long ago friend of the family.

Though there are neither horse nor cow in the barn, there are evidences of their onetime occupancy. Prince's harness, complete with breeching, hangs from the wall. His halter and grain box are up overhead in the tie-up. The cow's stall has become a storage depot for plant pots, but her chain and can of Cowcare are there gathering dust.

The mow holds only a covering of hay but it is enough to give fragrance to the barn and to furnish chaff for the birds in winter. The carriage and the pung and sleigh have long been disposed of and their departure left room for domestic exiles from the house: the parlor airtight stove, wicker rockers, Grandma's dining table, and a spool bed.

Everywhere in the barn are belongings of my relatives, even of Great-grandfather Friend whose adze and flail and porgy kettle are among my prized possessions. An oversize soap box is filled with normal school books, lesson plans, and sketch books—relics of Aunt Fannie's days of teaching. Hanging from the beams are two handwoven baskets made by my Great-grandfather Grindle.

My possessions are among those of my forebears: a turf cutter, a lawnmower and a brightly painted garden cart. Boxes are filled with college notebooks and catalogues and momentos.

I like to think that my Friend's Corner barn has not changed. But I have the suspicion that it is fast becoming a curiosity shop.

Spare rooms

The farmhouses of my childhood at Friend's Corner were homes of eight or nine rooms with adjoining sheds that led to commodious hay-filled barns. The downstairs rooms were often shabby from continual use, but upstairs one room, reserved for the use of occasional guests, was spotless and unscarred. This was designated as the "spare room." Its door was shut; its shades were drawn. Less frequently used than the parlor, it came to have an aura of sanctity.

The spare room in my home changed status when I was old enough to be left in the care of my mother's younger sister. Aunt Fannie occupied the room when she came to stay with me. Her visits became so frequent that she came to leave some of her belongings in the spare room. The room lost its air of inviolability; its door was open; its shades were raised; it became "Aunt Fannie's room."

Great-aunt Fan had two guest chambers which she designated as the "west spare" and the "south spare." She would have been more accurate had she called them the "west storage" and the "south storage."

The west room was a glorified clothes closet. On the beds were hats: winter hats and summer hats, felt hats and flowered hats, fur turbans and sunbonnets. Aunt loved hats and she could seldom bring herself to part with one. Her shoes were carefully paired along one wall. Her parasols and umbrellas were tilted in a corner. Scarfs and gloves were carefully sorted into neat piles on top of the bureau.

The south room was used as a storage chamber of a very different nature. In that room were piled the back issues of the *Delineator*, the *American*, the *Geographic* and the *Youth's Companion*. When our family spent Sunday with Great-aunt, as we often did, my cousins and I were told after dinner, "Now you children go up to the south spare and make yourselves right at home." In the mid-afternoon she paid us a call and she did not come empty-handed. A pan of apples or a plate of cookies was placed on the floor beside the absorbed readers.

Grandmother Maddocks's spare room was the ultimate in spare rooms. The sun was seldom allowed to shine on its marble-topped bureau; its bed was covered with a knit spread and its pillows were draped with embroidered shams. Feet seldom touched the button rugs scattered on the straw matting. No clothing was stored there; no magazines were piled there. The room was sparingly decorated. On the west wall was a cross-stitched motto; on the bureau, a cologne bottle and pin tray of pink glass. On the shelf were candlesticks and a luster pitcher.

Usually guests occupied the "back bedroom," a smaller and less austere bedroom. Uncle Vern, Grandfather's younger brother, was invited to sleep in the spare room. He came every four or five years to visit his numerous brothers and sisters in Maine. He came from Seattle and took pride in his worn and battered suitcase that he said had crossed the continent a dozen times. Everyone knew that he used the worn case from choice. His diamond stickpin, his tailor-made suit and his fancy fedora bespoke his prosperity and love of good clothes.

Uncle Vern owned a six-story livery stable where the horses of the American Express Company were boarded. I wondered if he wore his stickpin and the fedora to the stable but I never plucked up courage to ask him. We knew that he must be a very important man because he was allowed to nap in the spare room without removing the spread or the shams. On occasion he smoked a cigar in Grandma's cherished room. But his stories were so numerous, his delight in being with his own people so obvious and his gifts so generous that even Grandma overlooked the sacrilege done to her spare room.

The firkins stored in the attic of our shed chamber are reminders that eastern Maine was once bound to the West Indies by a trade that featured "ventures" and lumber, "long sweetening" and sugar.

The firkins belonged to my paternal grandfather who in the years before the Civil War sailed to Caribbean ports in his schooner *Meridian*, laden with Ellsworth or Bangor or Portland lumber. Grandfather always had room on the deck or in the hold for "ventures" sent by neighbors or friends who sought to make a few dollars by sending surplus goods to West Indian cities. These were boxes of turnips and parsnips; crates of hens and geese, which must have made a noisy cargo; bags of potatoes and Ben Davis apples, always "good keepers"; butter in brine-filled crocks; and firkins filled with cheeses, some plain and others flavored with sage or caraway.

Grandfather usually made two West Indies voyages in a year, the first one in November or December, the second in February or March, each trip being of about eight weeks duration. On the return trip the hold was filled with hogsheads of "long sweetening," as molasses was then called, and with boxes of sugar. The sweet cargo was bound for Brown's Sugarhouse, one of the largest refineries in New England and the most impressive structure on the Portland waterfront.

But Grandfather's return cargo was not limited to Portland-bound goods. He brought luxuries for Rockland and other ports on the homeward journey. There were bags of fragrant coffee beans, boxes of oranges, and firkins of figs and raisins. My father recalled that, when as a child he "wished on a star," his wish was always for sweet chocolate brought from the Indies by his captain father. The captain seldom disappointed his son.

My firkins are also reminders that the cooperage craft once flourished in eastern Maine, where every town had at least one cooper. Some towns had three followers of the trade: a wet cooper, a dry cooper, and a white cooper. The wet cooper made casks and hogsheads to hold rum and molasses. He was often a traveler. It saved schooner space to transport the staves to the Indies and to take along a cooper to assemble the Maine staves into waterproof containers for the return voyage.

The dry coopers, more often stay-at-homes, made firkins. From shooks they also made boxes that were used and reused in the West Indies trade.

The white cooper was regarded as the elite of the trade. He made grain measures—pint, quart, peck, and bushel containers. He turned out beautiful wooden utensils for the kitchen, knife and fork holders, spice boxes, and stirring spoons. In Father's childhood the white cooper was one of the first pedlars to show up after the roads had settled from mud time. Father recalled that cooper Snow often put up for the night at Captain Wood's saltwater farm, where the pedlar's wagon loaded with wooden ware filled the barn with forest fragrance. Father had a good reason to remember the cooper because every spring he gave father a gift, the product of his nimble fingers. One year, it was a pair of stilts; another, a baseball bat; once, a diminutive chest of drawers which is still cherished as a momento of the days when craftsmanship in wood was common in seaboard towns.

Every November I give the firkins an annual outing. I select a warm and sunny day for the chore and one of the boys in the neighborhood brings the firkins from the shed attic to the back porch where I remove the lids and set them in the air for a day of sunning. When I take off the lids, I imagine that I smell the fragrance of coffee and the spice of caraway and sage.

Some of the firkins are so old that cracks have appeared in their sides and the lids no longer fit. These, at the end of the day, are stored under the barn bench for winter keeping. When spring brings soft rain and damp fog, I transfer the ailing firkins to the corner of the porch, where a few days in the salty dampness restore them to their former state of tightness.

maine pastures

Pastures are disappearing in eastern Maine. Where cows and horses once grazed there now grow hardhack and juniper, poplars and birches. Some pastures are completely wood-grown with firs and spruces and pines.

In my childhood I was familiar with four pastures. I knew the pasture of the White Granite Company, where on "off days" four great white horses cropped the grass. On work days they pulled the galamander that drew the granite from the quarry to the cutting sheds. Every day goats grazed in the pasture. Rumor had it that Mr. White had imported them from Montana. They were constant nibblers and kept the alders from growing. I never went into the pasture because I feared the goats with their sharp, twisted horns but I liked to press against the wire fence and call to them. Though they raised their heads, they never approached me. I believed that they longed for the mountains of Montana. I called them "Mr. White's homesick goats."

A quarter of a mile from our home place was the Slaven pasture where all summer long five cows fed. Every morning we could hear the ding-dong of their bells. Afternoons, when they rested in the shade, their bells were muted. The sound of the bells gave an indication of the direction of the wind—when the wind blew from the south, the sound of the bells was clearest. Mother allowed me to go to the Slaven pasture only in the company of an adult. When our neighbor, Annie Treworgy, went there to pick blueberries, I was her glad companion. She wore a "peanut hat" to protect her face and she drew long black stockings (with feet cut off) over her arms and wrists. I wore no hat and my arms were bare. In the hot sun I could almost feel the freckles pop out on my nose and arms. When we had filled our pails with berries, Annie carefully removed the leaves and green berries from the top of her pail. She called this process "deaconing." My father was a deacon of the Baptist Church and I was not pleased with Annie's nomenclature.

It was in August that we children went most often to Uncle's pasture. We went not to pick berries but to seek out dried, round growths that when squeezed gave out puffs of spores which resembled smoke. We called them "smoke bombs" and used them in pasture warfare.

It was the home pasture with which I was most familiar. Daily we looked across it to the blue waters of the bay. We led the cow and Prince there to feed. Father and I picked berries there. Olive and I "played poison" there. (We jumped from one rock to another. The child who slipped and touched the ground was declared "poisoned.") We went to the pasture to gather wild flowers: roses in June, hardhack and meadowsweet in July, asters and goldenrod in September. We followed the curving pasture brook to the shore.

We spent most of our time playing on the ledges. When we were very young, Mother required that we play on the flat, moss-covered ledges near the house. There we set up housekeeping with broken dishes and leaking pans. When we were older, we were allowed to play on larger ledges that were distant from the house. These sloped to the shore and were lichen-covered. We had outgrown keeping house; we enacted the life of an imaginary family, the Sopers. There was the father, a rich businessman, and the mother who had once been an opera singer. The oldest daughter, Dorothy, was a nurse. The sons, Walter and John, went to Yale and Harvard. There were two little sisters, teenaged May and sweet Dolly. Olive and I played either female or male roles. In fact, we often played two or three roles at the same time. Neither of us liked to play May, whom we had created as a namby-pamby. The life of the Soper family gave our imagination full play. Such misfortunes the family suffered: fire and shipwreck, burglary and sickness. We were innocent and knew nothing of the moral horrors that vex the TV families of today. We never allowed our characters to die, though we were several times tempted to arrange May's demise.

When we tired of our make-believe characters, we took the parts of summer people whom we admired. Olive chose to be Madam Slaven with lots of money, or Mrs. Abbott who had been a missionary to India. I liked to be Mrs. Emily Loring who wrote books, or Mrs. Mary Curtis, a beloved neighbor who every winter sent me books from the Old Corner Bookstore.

Every few years I have the saplings and bushes in the pasture cut down. This is the year the chore must be done. I sometimes play with the idea of importing some Montana goats to keep the area free of bushes but I am sure that the idea is not practical. I am too old to care for the goats. I could not afford to pay a man to tend them even if I could find one. Shepherds and goatherds are indeed in short supply in eastern Maine.

the home brook

Our home brook that drained the woodland swamp, meandered through the meadow, and plunged down the pasture incline to the bay gave my cousins and me great joy in all seasons of the year. In June we gathered strawberries on its banks; in August we waded in its cool pools; in October we gathered bright leaves and beechnuts from the trees that grew beside it; in winter we skated on its white expanse.

But it was in spring that we enjoyed it most. In March it was our path to the maple grove where Father bored holes in a dozen trees, inserted wooden spiles that he had whittled, and placed a bucket under each. We waited for the bittersweet sap to collect in the containers and then we each took a drink. Father made a toast, "Here's to an early spring with no surprise snowstorms and no late frosts." My cousins and I were expected to empty each bucket every afternoon. My mother had the hardest chore—boiling down the sap in a great kettle on the back of the Home Clarion stove. The task necessitated a hot fire and resulted in a steam-filled room.

Before the sap season was over we saw signs of spring in the brook. Early in April the ice seemed to pull away from the edge of the brook, and it became honeycombed with holes. After a warm day the ice disappeared. When the runoff from the snow combined with a spring rain, our little brook became a miniature torrent, and rapids and eddies appeared. Sometimes the narrow, rock lined course below the meadow bridge could not carry away the water and suddenly we had a pond in the field.

When the water subsided and the brook was back in its usual channel we liked to follow its course from swamp to shore and to look for the first growing things of the season: green balls of skunk cabbages and clumps of pussy willows. We avoided the cabbages but we gathered great armfuls of the pussy willows for Mother, who massed them in a vase for the top of the parlor whatnot.

As April gave way to May, we followed the brook to seek out the first wild flowers. We found the arbutus, fragrant under its browned leaves. Later we found wood sorrel and Canada mayflowers. In the meadow we picked violets, the delicately scented white ones and the long stemmed purple violets that grew in the peat moss. In the pasture we found the swaying wild oats and the belled claytonia.

It was in late May that we went looking for our favorites, the lady slippers and the jack-in-the-pulpits. Mother cautioned us not to pick the lady slippers but we delighted to take a census of them, counting the deep pink ones, the light pink ones and an occasional white one. We took no census of the "jacks" which were very numerous in the swamp. I believe that our chief interest in them came from the hazards involved in finding them. We had to leap from one swamp hummock to another with the exciting chance of stepping into the water.

The apple trees that grew beside the brook gave their own late testimony of the spring. The wildings in the woods blossomed first, their frail white flowers touched with pink. When the bellflower tree by the bridge blossomed, it was just as though someone had thrown a pink blanket over it. We liked to sit under the blossom-covered boughs. While we listened to the humming of the bees, we fashioned crowns and necklaces with flowers we plucked from the tree. Father used to warn us not to pick too many blossoms, "Take care not to snip off too many flowers. The blooming bellflower tells us that spring is nearly over and that it is time to look ahead to summer and to fall with the harvest of apples."

Our home brook was more than a playground for my cousins and me. It was our barometer for the coming and going of spring.

more than meets the eye

"Why do you always write about what you see on your walks? Don't you also hear?" asked one of my friends.

Her query set me to taking note of the sounds that I hear when I walk on the private road to Slaven's. It is one of my favorite walks. The road is not blacktopped; there is little traffic. The roadsides have a succession of wild flowers from the starflowers and trilliums of spring to the asters and goldenrod of fall; birds nest in the trees that edge the road. The hillside curve gives a view of the Bay and Long Island, with Newbury Neck and Mount Desert in the distance.

During August I have heard varied sounds: the purr of cars and the clatter of cycles on the main road; the laughter of Eva's grandchildren at play; the thump of the ball against the backboard as Mike and Tom practice; the sound of sweet music from Thorpe's and Keller's; the querulous call of the gulls; the *tap tap tap* of woodpeckers seeking worms in dead trees; the call of songbirds; the distant barking of Beau demanding his supper. One Sunday morning when the air was very clear and the wind was from the west, I heard the ringing of the church bells at the Head-of-the-Bay. The early afternoon onshore breeze brings in the sounds from the Bay: a sharp whistle and the starting gun for the sailing races. In the early evening I have heard the whine of a plane and the puttering of a "chopper."

My interest in sights and sounds has not kept me from noting scents. At low tide I catch the salty odor of the flats. On the shortcut at the curve there is a bank of sweet scented ferns that fills the air with fragrance. When Prim runs through the bayberry or the sweet fern, the shrubs give off a spicy sweetness. One night a truck loaded with baled hay passed me and left the lingering smell of meadow. When I stop at my neighbor's roadside garden I breathe the fragrance of her flowering stock.

In the last few days I have enjoyed some taste sensations. I have eaten round sweet blueberries and large red raspberries that grow along the road. I have sampled the purplish-pink berries of the wild pear; the flavor is delicious but the seeds are large and hard. I ate a few string cherries, but they were so sour that I was glad to leave them to the waxwings and catbirds who objected to my sampling of their food supply. I ate several bearberries; they are larger than blueberries and have less flavor. There have been blackberries on which to feast; they are large, luscious, and seeping with purple juice. I have nibbled at the puckery huckleberries. I ate a few bunchberries and so disproved the dictum of my childhood, "Bunchberries are poison." The berries are beautiful to see but are tasteless to eat. I picked a few greenish-red berries of the Canada mayflower and the plump purple berries of the clintonia but I refused to taste them. One has to draw the line somewhere even in pursuit of material for a column.

I hope that my friend will notice that I do more than see when I walk. I use my ears and my nose, and on occasion, I taste.

fall chores

I have been busy with my fall chores: pulling up annuals, cutting off the heads of the phlox and other perennials, treating the peonies to a feeding of bonemeal and removing the garden stakes. I had help in covering the roses with a triple blanket of dirt, hay, and brush. Kind helpers cut back the brush and brought it to the yard. I enjoy covering the flower borders and taking stock of the biennials and perennials. I know that some plants will survive the winter: the peonies, the phlox, thistles, painted daisies, feverfew, bee balm and day lilies. The coral bells, primroses and asters will get through the coldest winter. But I have doubts about the mums surviving. I am sure that most of the foxgloves will die.

Some of my chores are barn chores. The barn floor and the benches must be swept, the tools cleaned and greased. Trash must be collected for disposal. The plant pots should be cleaned and sorted according to size. Boxes must be stored up overhead.

Trapping will be one of my fall chores. I shall borrow Ralph Bowden's "keep-them-alive" trap and attempt to catch my squirrel, a red one who has lost the tip of his tail. In the spring and summer he was content to be the occupant of the shed and the barn. He went through the trash bags, gnawed the vegetables on the shed shelf and stole the bird seed. He acted as though he owned the premises. This fall he has taken to coming into the house. I have met him in the attic. In the night I hear him in the partition as he goes about his nocturnal chores. Often when I return from getting the mail, he is perched on the ridgepole of the house. The greeting he gives me is clear: "Why are you back? The house and barn and shed are very much better off without you and that black dog." If and when I catch the squirrel, I shall transport the trap to some thickly wooded section and let the animal free.

I enjoy doing the fall chores. But I know that they are not as practical and important as those that Father used to do.

Father banked the house. He first took the banking boards from up overhead in the grain room. He then upended them against the outside wall of the tie-up and carefully inspected them for loose boards and rotten wood. Some years he painted them white to match the house. He always chose a sunny afternoon for the banking chore.

Mother helped with the fall chores. She cut down the hollyhocks that grew at the end of the ell and pulled off the tops of the day lilies that grew under the parlor windows. On the north side of the house Father covered the foundation with hay before he nailed the boards in place. Finally the boards were placed against the house and covered with boughs of fir and spruce. At the windy corner of the house he set small evergreens in the ground.

Mother played an important part in putting on the outside windows. She washed the outside of the house windows and washed and polished the panes of glass in the outside windows. Sometimes I helped her. I soon tired of the work and became bored; I was glad to act on her suggestion, "Why don't you go and see what your Cousin Olive is doing?"

In late October Father took the dahlia bulbs down cellar. These were sorted into three boxes. One was marked "yellow"; the second was marked "quill"; the third was unmarked and held the bulbs of the pink and white dahlias that Mother did not hold in high regard. The dahlias joined the apples, carrots, potatoes, beets, and turnips that had been cellar stored in September.

There were some winter foods that Mother did not trust to storage in the cellar. The pumpkins and the squashes and the cranberries had had a long fall of drying on the back porch. In the daytime they basked in the sunshine; on cold nights they were covered with blankets. Mother prepared a winter keeping place for them in the ell chamber, a sunny room that was warmed by the kitchen chimney. Father, Mother, and I moved the "pie fodder" to the bedroom, placed squashes and pumpkins on papers spread on the floor, pushed the cranberries into a cool corner and covered them all with a plaid red blanket—one that I now use on my bed. I'm always hoping that it will give me dreams of cranberry sauce and pumpkin pie.

The big pots of mums were the last fall residents on the porch. Every evening Father brought them into the dining room; every morning he returned them to the porch. Finally, when the flowers had faded, Mother said, "John, won't you take the pots of mums down cellar? They are the last of my garden." I know just how she felt. As I write in early November there are a few frayed flowers left in the garden; a campanula still waves its blue bells.

In all of Father's winter preparations he did not forget the horse, the cow, and the hens. He got out Prince's winter blankets, the older one for stall-standing and the newer one for street-standing. Father chinked the windows of the horse stall and the tie-up with crocus bags. He banked the henhouses with boughs.

The final chore was bringing in the winter woodboxes and the sitting room stove. The small oilcloth covered box used in the kitchen during the summer was banished to the woodshed and a large, varnished pine box took its place. The sitting room woodbox was a bushel basket made by Great-grandfather Grindle. Father had assistance in bringing the stove from the barn where it had spent the summer in retirement. Uncle Arthur or Dan or Cousin Herman came to help with the task they all disliked. There was always the danger of jamming a thumb or knocking the paint off a door frame or losing a leg off the stove. Mother supervised the move and gave frequent suggestions. My cousins and I hovered around and half hoped for a misadventure. Old Joe and Uncle Arthur's Don-dog were often present for the fall spectacular.

In early November they started singing Thanksgiving hymns at the church services. The one that my father sang with the greatest vigor was the one with the words,

> all is safely gathered in
> ere the winter's storms begin.

I could tell by the smile on his face that he was thinking of the cranberries and the pumpkins, not of the sitting room stove.

setting a good table

I discovered recently that the expression "to set a good table" does not mean what it did sixty years ago when my great-aunts were in the flower of their housekeeping. Today a woman is said to set a good table if she serves bacon for breakfast, tossed salad and chops for lunch, french fries and steak for dinner. In my great-aunts' day the phrase did not refer to the menu but to the table setting.

Sixty years ago a housewife who set a good table covered her dining table with a square of linen. My great-aunts had numerous linens—everyday ones, second-best ones, and best ones that were hemstitched and so long they nearly touched the carpet. Every cloth, whether ivy or tulip or daisy or rose, had matching napkins.

The use of a linen cloth presented a problem: how often should it be changed? Aunt Georgia and Aunt Maria guarded against too frequent changes by protecting the covering with tray cloths which could be easily removed when soiled. Aunt Louise and Aunt Fan used the same process but in reverse; when a spot appeared on the linen they covered it with a cloth. Aunt Mary's tablecloth was always unprotected and it was changed every Wednesday and every Saturday whether it was spotted or spotless.

A handsome addition to the linen-spread table were the silver napkin rings, usually engraved with the owner's name. Aunt Fan's bore the inner inscription, "Gift of Brother Vern." Aunt Mary's ring was completely circled by her name, Mary Esther Maddocks Burrill. The rings were kept shining by daily wiping with whiting and a soft cloth.

Near the center of the table the aunts kept a silver spoon-holder and a castor with its bottles for oil and vinegar and its shakers for salt and pepper. Beside the hostess's place was a cut glass water pitcher and a semicircle of glasses. There was a great domed butter dish with its inner glass plate. The plate of butter was removed to the cool cellarway when a meal was over, but the silver covering was left on the table, an emblem, as it were, of the family's prosperity. I recall vividly Aunt Fan's indictment of her younger sister, "Georgia sets a good table except that the butter dish is always soiled." She was always critical of her youngest sister, whose sewing machine was near the dining table. "Louise," she complained, "treats her dining table as an adjunct to the sewing machine; pins in the cloth, shears beside the castor and a paper pattern over the spoon holder."

Each of my great-aunts had three sets of dishes, white ironware for everyday, a mail-order set for second best, and a Sunday set, which in the case of Aunt Fan and Aunt Mary was Haviland. The Sunday set was complete from platters to butter chips, from gravy bowl to soup tureen. All the sets had curved, elongated vessels, known as bone dishes, that were set beside the dinner plates to hold potato parings, discards of meat and fish, and corncobs.

Whether Aunt Fan set the table with ironware or with Haviland, she placed a special cup at Uncle Pearl's place. He was proud of his appearance and he chose to use a cup whose inner shelf protected his twirled black mustache from stain.

On the top shelves of their china closets the aunts kept dishes that were used on special days: tall chocolate pots with matching cups and saucers, tall pedestal cake plates, nut bowls, celery vases, soup tureens, and pickle jars with a special fork attached.

Each of my great-aunts had a special flourish in setting a good table. Aunt Maria filled the butter dish with fresh butter for each meal. And such butter—golden yellow, churned and molded into pats in Aunt's own buttery. Aunt Georgia, the only city-dweller among the five sisters, kept on her table a silver bowl filled with native New England fruit in summer and fall, imported pears and oranges and pineapples in winter and spring.

Aunt Louise kept a majolica pitcher on her table. In spring and summer it was filled with garden flowers, in fall with begonia blossoms and fragrant leaves picked from her house plants.

The R. F. D. man delivered the mail at the Burrill house just before dinner. It was Aunt Mary's habit to bring the papers and the letters to the table when she served the dessert. While Uncle Earnest ate his piece of pie Aunt read aloud to him.

Aunt Fan's flourish was one that I found both endearing and convenient. At noontime and supper time she set an extra plate at the table in the happy expectation that a niece would come in to share a meal.

When I was a child I was proud that my great-aunts set tables splendid with linen and sparkling with silver and glass that bespoke prosperity and thrift. Now that I have become a woman, gratitude has displaced pride. I am grateful that when my aunts set a good table, they spread the cloth of love.

Keeping house plants

Singing in the choir runs in some families; collecting antiques, in others. Keeping house plants runs in mine.

My five great-aunts, spirited sisters who disagreed on politics, investments, and church affiliation, were as one in their devotion to the cultivation of house plants. That is not to say that they cultivated them in the same manner.

Aunt Louise and Aunt Maria were scatterers. Plants were everywhere in their homes. Parlor mantel, pantry shelves, and marble-topped tables all had their plants. Aunt Georgia, who lived in a large city home such as befitted her prosperous storekeeper-husband, went in for impressive ferns and parlor maples grown in large brass pots and china jardinieres. Yearly transplanted by the florist, they grew and flourished as though they were symbols of the family's prosperity. Aunt Fan and Aunt Mary were able to consolidate their plants because they owned bulging bay windows which they filled with cascading growing things.

I was most familiar with Aunt Fan's display of plants because her dining table was set in the curve of the bay window. My father, who did not care for the proximity of food and foliage, often remarked to Mother, "I feel as though I were eating in a jungle when we have dinner at your Aunt Fan's." Mother was always unconcerned and she laughed when she said, "I notice that your feelings do not keep you from eating a second piece of pie."

Unlike my father, I liked looking at the plants while I ate. When the conversation turned to prices and politics, I entertained myself by counting the blossoms on the fuchsia and estimating the yardage of the ivy that festooned the window.

Mother followed the horticultural path so well trodden by her aunts. Like Aunt Maria and Aunt Louise, she scattered her plants about the house so that I was never surprised to confront a cactus in a corner or a petunia in the pantry. Like her Aunt Georgia, she had a Boston fern in a brass pot and parlor maple in a jardiniere. During the summer months, fern and maple dwelt in dignity in the parlor. But in the winter they were exiled from the unheated front room to sulk in the sitting room bay window in the plebian company of geraniums and begonias.

Mother did her five aunts one better. She had two plants that she called "my heirloom plants." My father took an interest in these because they had some connection with his family. One was a giant oleander grown from a slip taken from a plant his captain-father had once brought from South Carolina. Its glossy green leaves and fragrant rose-like blossoms made it one of the most handsome in Mother's collection. In the summer it sunned itself on the front porch. In the winter it had the monopoly of the dining room's most sunny window. The second was a calla lily inherited from Father's Aunt Hannah. Mother repotted the bulb every third year, washed the foliage every week and was rewarded every March with waxy white flowers.

I, too, have followed the family tradition of raising house plants but circumstances have limited my cultivation. In the summer I have been at Friend's Corner; in the winter, in a village across the state. Every June some plants go to the country for the summer; every fall some return to the village for the winter. I pride myself on my skill in packing my plants for the cross-state journey. I water each one well, wrap each in newspaper, and set it erect in a box or basket. The trunk of my car can hold a surprising number of plants—between two and three dozen.

Mindful that the interior of the trunk becomes hot on a warm day, I break the journey for my plants by a pause in the shade and a lifting of the trunk cover. The plants usually make the trip safely. When a limb or a top is broken, I carefully root it in water and have another plant.

Keeping plants runs in my family. But I claim that I am the first to keep plants on the go.

uncle octave's coot stew

When Uncle Octave married Aunt Hannah and came to Friend's Corner to live, he was regarded as somewhat of a foreigner by the Maine-born people of the neighborhood. Uncle did his best to divest himself of evidences of his French-Canadian background; he changed his name to one of Yankee origin, selected by Aunt Hannah; he seldom used his native tongue.

While he was at the granite yard, he loved to talk about the Canadian food of his childhood. He delighted in French cooking and Aunt Hannah mastered Uncle's family recipes. She became an expert at making crepes and "province pastry." Uncle's Yankee friends came to like the rich egg batter fried in deep fat and the hearty pork pies.

One day at work Uncle heard the lonely call of a coot and exclaimed, "That reminds me that I have not tasted a coot for over twenty years. There's nothing better than a coot stew."

His cutter companions laughed and one of them said, "There never was a coot stew made that could be eaten with relish, and you very well know it, Octave."

Uncle vowed that some Sunday he would make a coot stew, bring it to the yard on Monday, warm it at the blacksmith's forge and give them all a treat.

For the next few days there was a great deal of joking about coot stew. That very Saturday, after supper, Uncle Octave took his gun and went to the shore. In a few hours he returned with three coot which he dry-picked while they were still warm.

Sunday morning, when he brought the birds to the kitchen to cook them, he was routed by Aunt Hannah. "Never will coot be cooked on my kitchen stove. If you must cook them, cook them in the backyard."

Uncle vowed that some Sunday he would make a coot stew, bring it to the yard on Monday, warm it at the blacksmith's forge and give them all a treat.

going. The coot and the turnips were put in the bubbling cauldron. For all his long life Phil recalled how the schoolroom was filled with a rank odor that suggested rotting seaweed and dead clams.

At noontime when Uncle picked a bit of the meat from a wing and tasted it, he made a grimace of distaste. He took the kettle from the stove, carried it outside, and poured the contents on a flat ledge back of the schoolhouse. When the coot had cooled, he picked the bones, carefully saving the bones and the bills and brushing the meat into a wide crack in the ledge.

"Let's go home to dinner," he said to his son, "Say nothing about this to your mother. We'll try again next Sunday."

The following Saturday Uncle invited Philip to ride to North Blue Hill with him. He assured Aunt Hannah that he was going there to buy a new rooster at the Dahlquist farm. He also bought a Bantam rooster and two hens, which were placed in a box on the journey home, then carefully concealed behind the schoolhouse door. "Your mother is to know nothing about this," said the father to his son.

After supper, as on the preceding Saturday, Uncle Octave went to the shore on the pretext of shooting coot, but actually he dug a peck of clams.

On Sunday morning Uncle and Philip left early for the schoolhouse, carrying a kettle with the clams and an axe concealed in a market basket. After a fire was built in the schoolhouse stove, the clams were put on to boil and Uncle killed, picked, and drew the Bantams. Then he gave them a long, slow cooking in the clam water. When the water cooled, Uncle removed the meat from the bones and pushed the bones down the same crack where he had disposed of the coot flesh. The bantam meat was returned to the clam water and the bones and bills of the coot were added. Uncle tasted the meat with satisfaction, gave a sample to his son and declared, "Don't taste a bit like chicken."

Uncle was delighted with his "coot stew," for which he begged an onion, salt and two quarts of milk. When the ingredients had been added, Aunt Hannah consented to sample the stew. She exclaimed, "This is delicious. I can't think that it was made from coot."

"Look at the bones and the beaks if you doubt me," was her husband's clinching reply.

The men at the granite yard were as surprised and mystified as was Aunt Hannah. Uncle's coot stew became a byword at Friend's Corner, but Uncle never attempted to duplicate his culinary masterpiece. Aunt Hannah remained a doubting Thomas and was often heard to remark, "I don't believe that Octave made that stew from coot."

The following summer Aunt Hannah met Farmer Dahlquist at the general store. The North Blue Hill farmer greeted her cheerfully and said, "Octave must have quite a flock of Bantams by now. Those were three fine birds I sold him last spring."

Aunt Hannah never faced her husband with the accusation that he used Bantams in the stew, but whenever the expression "coot stew" was used in her hearing, she sniffed and exclaimed, "Coot hoax."

back porch politics

In my childhood the men of the neighborhood gathered on our back porch to talk politics on summer evenings. Daniel Treworgy, our nearest neighbor, came first and he selected the west corner of the hammock for his evening location. Father chose the other corner. Uncle Arthur, Father's older brother, sat in the captain's chair and smoked his pipe, providing a smoke screen against the mosquitoes and black flies of June and July. Cousin Herman, the last to arrive, seated himself on the big granite step. He was the only Democrat in the group. When I was very small, I used to think that his lowly place was emblematic of the status of his political party.

Cousin Herman held his own against the three Republicans. He was sharp enough to sow the seeds of discord between the brothers. On occasion he brought cartoons he had made: sketches of a toothy Roosevelt or an overfat Taft or a bellicose Root. Dan never took part in the debates. When he was challenged he always said, "I think just as John does." Now and then one of my cousins ran to the porch with the plea, "Uncle John, come and play a round or two of hide-and-seek with us. You always do." Finally, he joined the children. His brother remarked, "When John finds he is losing an argument, he goes to play with the young ones."

In August Cousin Herman got a valuable reinforcement. His older brother, who ran a business college and a diploma shop in Rockland, came for a visit. Cousin Henry was well-read and well-traveled. He was hesitant in his speech and spoke softly, but with authority, and held to his views with all the pugnacity of a bulldog with a bone. When his brother and his uncles, all younger than he, had had their say, he made a summation for the Democratic cause. I respectfully recall some of his dicta: the tariff should be lowered; Teddy Roosevelt talks loudly but he busts few trusts; the United States should be a member of the League of Nations.

Nineteen-twelve was the year back porch political ranks were broken. Father and his brother Arthur became Progressives and ardent supporters of Roosevelt for president. When Cousin Henry came for his annual visit, he quoted the humorist, "All that is left for Teddy and Taft to do is to count the funeral bouquets."

The Wood Brothers later returned to the G.O.P. but their Republicanism was never the same. Father had good words for Al Smith as well as for Coolidge, a few good words for Harding, none for Hoover and Dewey. He and Cousin Henry were as one in their approval of Wilson and F.D.R.

The talkers on the porch had topics other than politics. The crops and the weather, the berry harvest and the mackerel run were also discussed. In 1912 they told and retold the saga of the sinking of the *Titanic*. In 1915 they talked of the sinking of the *Lusitania* and argued the culpability of the captain; they questioned the judgment of the Americans in sailing on the Cunard liner and suggested that the liner had carried shells.

The *Lusitania* story greatly impressed my cousins and me and we often reenacted the disaster. Uncle's spreading Greening apple tree in the lower field took the part of the liner. The "passengers" lay on the lower limbs with the "captain" astride an upper limb shouting directions to an imaginary crew, "No zig-zagging; straight ahead for land."

The child who played the exciting role of the German sub hid behind the rock wall with a cedar pole in hand. Suddenly the sub came toward the liner. The bomb (the cedar pole) struck the liner. In a shower of leaves and green apples the passenger and captain tumbled out into the sea of green grass. At once they underwent a change of roles and became exploding shells. Each of us seized kettles hidden in the grass and beat on them with stones. The Greening was out of sight of the house so Aunt Nellie and Uncle Arthur never witnessed the "sinking of the *Lusitania*." Aunt Nellie did inquire about the kettles missing from the shed and Uncle commented, "I can't understand why my Greening tree has lost so many apples and leaves." We children understood.

My cousins and I grew up to take a keen interest in politics. I am sure that our interest was nurtured by listening to the back porch discussions of our elders.

The Village

shopping at the grange store

Some of the earliest memories of my childhood are of going to the Grange Store with my father. Mother seldom went with us, though she helped pack the eggs and the butter into the wagon or the pung, depending upon the season. She never failed to caution Father, "Keep your mind on your trading and get the best prices you can." When we were ready to start she handed Father the store book in which the storekeeper would record our purchases and list the articles that we had brought to trade. As we drove out of the yard she called, "Now, John, you buy only the items on my list. And you watch Esther."

He called back, "Yes, Lizzie, yes, indeed I will."

It was all a drama of words. Mother knew very well that Father would buy candy for me, a gift for her. She well knew that "watching Esther" to my father meant allowing me to do anything I liked within the bounds of safety.

It was a one mile drive to the Grange Store. Father let me hold the reins and take the whip out of the whipstock though no one ever touched Prince with it. Father used to say, "The whip is for show and not for blow." Father enlivened the trip by talking. He told about the work at the Granite; he reviewed his Sunday School lesson; he conjectured about the crops and the weather. I did not understand all that he said but his voice was pleasant and comforting. Now and then to be companionable I asked a question. I knew just what he would say when we crossed the bridge over McHard's Stream: "When my father's schooner *Meridian* was built here, her bowsprit stretched out way above the bridge."

When we reached the store Father fastened Prince to one of the wooden hitching posts. In winter he covered Prince with a blanket; in fly season he threw a protecting netting over him. I hurried ahead to open the door while either Mr. Long, the store's proprietor, or his son Ross came out to help Father unload the butter and eggs.

While Father did the trading I entertained myself. I waked the orange tiger cat who slept on a bolt of calico; I pulled out the drawers of the thread chest and admired the colors; I dipped my finger into an open pail of peanut butter. If it were winter, I approached the box stove that was always red-hot, and with my back to my father and the storekeepers, I spat on the stovetop. I congratulated myself on the accuracy of my aim and the absence of my mother. I reached my arm into the bean bin and gave the Jacob's Cattle a good stirring. When I was done with the stirring, I took out a handful of the beans and threw a few on top of the hot stove to watch them curl up and burn. I dropped others into the brine of the pickle barrel and listened for the faint plops. If Mr. Long or Ross went to the back room to draw molasses or vinegar from the hogsheads stored there, I was sure to tag along and request, "Dribble a little 'lasses on my hand, please."

My circuit of the store always ended at the candy case, where I pressed my nose against the glass. I waited for my father to come stand beside me and say, "Well, Daughter, you have been such a good little girl that you may have ten cents worth of candy. You name it, and it is yours."

It was never easy for me to "name it." How could one choose between Boston baked beans and jawbreakers, between ice cream drops and peppermints? I couldn't, and it ended with Father saying to Ross, "I'll spend another dime. Give her a sample of everything."

After we had made our purchases my father asked me, "Now, what shall we buy for your mother?" He always vetoed my suggestion of a box of chocolates or a bag of "boughten cookies." The gift was usually percale or toweling or a piece of lace.

Our final chore was in the grain room. Father backed the wagon (or pung, if it were winter) to the door of the storage place where Ross stood ready to load the meal or the middlings or the bran into the back of the vehicle.

As we left the village, Father would again mention the bowsprit of *Meridian.* Our journey home was always a swift one because Prince was eager for his home stall, his hay, and his measure of cracked corn.

a sunday school concert

The Sunday School concert was an important event of my childhood Christmases.

Soon after Thanksgiving I started to memorize my recitation, sometimes assigned by the Sunday School teacher but more often chosen by Mother from the *Popular Reader,* a large gray-bound book that contained plays, songs, dialogues, monologues, and recitations for both children and adults. The first few pages of the book fascinated me. They showed pictures of a woman clad in a togalike gown. Under each picture was the name of an emotion; love, hate, fear, distrust, and all the others. The women by lips, eyes, face, and hands depicted each feeling. My pieces were happy ones. I took care to model my expression and gestures on those of the elocutionist when, according to the caption, she was depicting "joy."

Both Father and Mother heard me recite my piece but they gave different directions. "Speak good and loud so that everyone can hear you," directed my mother. My father's advice was, "Hold your chin up, your shoulders back and look your hearers right in the eye."

After my piece was learned I delighted to repeat it to the neighbors. By Christmas week everyone knew "Esther's recitation" by heart and was heartily sick of it.

The Sunday School teachers and a few of the mothers met early in December to make and stuff the candy bags. They made the bags of red cotton netting. They popped corn for them and marked each with the name of a child. Later candy was added.

Mrs. Lena Snow, our Sunday School superintendent, bought the ribbon candy for the bags from Max Hinckley, the owner of the general store. The teacher wanted to have enough candy. "I'm sure that twenty pounds will be ample," she said. Max liked to have her have more than enough. "Better make it twenty-two," he would say as he weighed the candy. After the candy had been poured into bags, Max carefully made out the bill to the Blue Hill Baptist Church Sunday School. Then he handed it to Mrs. Snow. She looked at it but before she could put it in her pocketbook, he said, "Please let me look at the bill again." He did more than look at it—he marked it "Paid."

The concert was on a weekday evening before Christmas. Now and then the roads were snow-covered so that we "punged" to the village. More often we had a bare Christmas so we drove to town in the carriage.

Mrs. Snow presided over the presentation of dialogues, songs and recitations. She knew just how to handle a little girl who broke into tears when she was called to the platform to speak her piece. She knew how to handle the little boys who pushed and pinched their companions. After a collection for the orphanage at Kodiak, Alaska we "had the tree."

A large fir decked with strings of popcorn and cranberries stood to the right of the altar. After the concert Mrs. Snow gave the signal for Santa's arrival. "Will someone please open the door to the vestibule? I heard the bells of Santa's reindeer a few minutes ago."

Santa was always there and he entered with much ha-ha-ha-ing and ringing of bells. One of Mrs. Snow's older sons played the role of Santa. If Bert played the part, Santa laughed so much and told so many stories that Mrs. Snow had to hurry him on his way. If Ed was Santa things went like clockwork so that before we knew it Santa was running out of the room with the call, "Goodnight, folks. I've got to hurry. I'm due in North Penobscot in twenty minutes."

Each Sunday School pupil received three gifts: a candy bag, a gift from the Sunday School teacher, and a gift brought by his parents and carefully marked with his name. For several years I was amazed that Santa's writing was so much like my mother's.

When the concert was over I was very happy. My gifts had pleased me; the sight of Santa had excited me. But I had one regret—I had not been asked to join any of the singing groups. (Monotones were of course not included.) When I mentioned my disappointment to my parents they were quick to console me. Mother did not hesitate to stretch the truth, "You spoke your piece the best of anyone."

My father added the postscript, "You certainly spoke the loudest of all."

recollections of hats

In the days of my childhood every Maine village had a millinery shop. Blue Hill's was owned by Miss Emma Osgood, who every spring and fall went to Boston to buy her seasonal supply of hats and to purchase flowers, ribbons, feathers, fruits, and veiling. Miss Osgood not only sold hats but she retrimmed old hats. Under her skillful fingers the hats underwent such a metamorphosis that the owners themselves did not recognize them.

Miss Osgood was a telephone operator as well as a milliner. The switchboard for the town phone service was in the corner of her shop. It was evident that she placed the desires of her hat customers ahead of the demands of the phone users. Judge Chase, the village lawyer whose office was in the Pendleton House across from Miss Osgood's store, did not bear her neglect with patience. When there was no answer to his crank-made call, he went to the office window and looked across to the Osgood shop. When he saw the phone operator fitting a customer with a beflowered hat, he was very annoyed. The Judge knew how to "send a message to Garcia." He dispatched one of his children with the order, "You tell Emma

Osgood to answer the phone this minute." If one of the little girls of the Chase family was the bearer of the message, her father's words were delivered with decorum. If a son were the messenger, he was sure to say, "Pa is awful mad. You had better answer him darned quick." Miss Osgood was never flustered. She sent a crisp reply to the Judge, "When I get this trimming basted into place, I'll attend to your father."

Grandmother, Aunt Fannie, and my mother did not buy hats from Miss Osgood. They, in fact, did not purchase hats. Grandmother's sister, Linda, was head trimmer in a West Roxbury hat shop. Every fall and spring she sent her sister a box of hats that had been used as patterns to guide the trimmers in their work. As the result of her generosity, her Blue Hill relatives were well hatted whatever the season.

Nor did my Great-aunt Fan buy hats from Miss Osgood. She fell heir to the hats of the three Owen Sisters who summered in her neighborhood. Each sister had a favorite color: Miss Bessie's was green, Miss Carrie's was purple, Miss Minnie's was blue. Aunt Fan set no value on green hats and she handed them on to anyone who could accept them. There were always takers. She cherished and admired and wore the blue ones and the purple ones. She had a bedroom that she called "my hat room." There she stored the creations from Philadelphia's most exclusive millinery emporium.

When Mother and I went to church we were proud to wear our Roxbury hats. I am sure that Mother's mind was on the sermon. Mine was not. I entertained myself by looking over the hats in the congregation. The four Merrill Sisters sat in front of us and I gazed at their Sunday raiment with no little admiration. I counted the roses on Mrs. Clay's hat and the bows on Mrs. McIntyre's turban. I twisted in my pew to see if Mrs. Snow had a new hat. She seldom had one because her interest lay in good works rather than new hats.

The hats that created the most interest in the Baptist Church were those worn by the village dentist's wife. Twice a year, in the spring and fall, the doctor and his wife went to Boston. Supposedly, he returned with dental supplies. Positively, she returned with hats. Her hats were high crowned, wide brimmed, and laden with flowers and fruits or velvet and feathers, according to the season. The doctor and his wife were usually late for church, and as they sat in a front pew, their entrance created no little stir. A rustle of excitement accompanied their progress up the center aisle and all the eyes in the congregation were centered on the new hat of the season. I recall that the minister once lost his place in the responsive reading when he saw a cherry-bedecked black hat bearing down on him.

I know of no Maine village that today has a millinery shop. I know of no woman who today has a bedroom devoted to her hats. And I know of no little girl who breaks the tedium of the church service by a survey of hats.

Church suppers

Church suppers are a New England institution. They fill the church coffers and they furnish food and fellowship for both the guests and the workers who put on the meals.

The secretary's book of the Blue Hill Baptist Church details the facts of the first church suppers. They were for members only and there was no charge. They followed an afternoon meeting of the ladies' Circle (and presumably came after the fathers had fed and milked the cows, fed the horses and the hens, and gathered up the children for the walk or ride to the home of the hostess.) A rule written in the record book specified the menu: "Bread and cheese, tea and milk, and loaves of cake." Each woman contributed according to the needs of her family. I suspect that nineteenth century Blue Hill hostesses were like those of today. I am sure every hostess would "happen to have on hand" a kettle of stew or a pot of beans.

Once, when the Circle met at the home of Mrs. Jairus Osgood, the young mothers left their babies to nap on Mrs. Osgood's pineapple bed. A woman with a sharp eye for money suggested that a fee of a penny be charged for a look at the five sleepers on the bed.

The wife of Dr. Alexander Fulton, who was herself a doctor and later, with her husband, the generous donor of the town clock, also earned money for the Circle. She had been to Paris and had learned to make cream puffs, a delicacy then unknown in eastern Maine. Mrs. Fulton came to the Circle with her basket filled with puffs and recipe slips. She charged ten cents for the combination, one confection and the rule for making it. Her wares were soon sold.

At my request, Miss Alwilda Osgood told me her recollections of church suppers in the late 1880s and 1890s. "We used to have one about every week when I was a child. The suppers were in the basement dining room of the chapel. I think that two women cooked the beans, the brown bread, and the white bread. They also brought the pickles. Everyone brought the desserts. I can remember Father loading Mother's things into a clothes basket and taking them to the chapel on the horse sled. In those days people brought cream pies galore. Mother made pastry, pies, and tarts. At first the suppers were free and then they charged ten cents. One man brought the Academy students who roomed in his house. He put in twenty-five cents for their suppers. The ladies did not like the idea too well."

My memories of church suppers go back for six decades. There must have been harvest suppers in the fall and strawberry festivals in June. These I do not recall. But I have vivid recollections of suppers on cold winter nights when eighty or ninety people were pressed into the small assembly room where the woodstove in the corner was quivering with heat. Adults seated themselves on long benches waiting the call to the dining room in the basement. At first we children were awed by the assembly of grown-ups and by the large-as-life pictures of former ministers staring down from the walls. Soon we forgot our elders and the pictures and began running and playing and hiding in the coat closet. When a parent intervened to quiet us, we children had a firm friend in Mrs. Snow, the supervisor of the Sunday School. She bustled to our defense: "Now I won't have the children scolded in the Lord's House. You children play all you want to but do take care not to run against the stove."

The children raced and played until Miss Lucy Billings appeared at the head of the stairs to nod to the minister that supper was ready. The minister went first, then the real old, then the rest by families. Father, Mother, and I were always at the end of the line because Father stayed to check the stove and to close the dampers. His cryptic remark was, "Don't want the building to burn down over our heads."

Either the minister or Mrs. Snow asked the blessing. I liked her blessings because they were always short. She knew how hungry we were and how quickly beans and brown bread cool.

After all the eating was over there was still food left. When Mother and I ventured into the kitchen to get her bean pot and pie plate, the ladies were busy dividing the leftovers: "Do take a few slices of Mrs. Wilfred's Grindle applesauce cake." "There is only a heel left from Florence Merrill's orange-raisin cake but it is well worth taking home." "Now take some of Miss Snow's doughnuts. They melt in your mouth."

The prices and menus of church suppers have changed in sixty years. But the important things are the same—the sociability and the sharing.

merrill & hinkley's store

The village store was a family business for almost a century. The first owners were Merrill Hinckley and Frank Merrill. There was no relationship although they shared a name.

I remember Frank Merrill well and I remember that my father used to say, "Mr. Merrill is a fine gentleman." I am sure my father's judgement was based on a consideration of Mr. Merrill's integrity and dignity. Mine was based on his being the father of the Merrill Sisters—girls who ranked high with me because of their talents and their style.

I never knew Merrill Hinckley but I have always heard tales about him and his dog. Usually the store dog was a Saint Bernard, one whose size was sure to discourage mischief-makers. One day a short-tempered man hurried up the steps to the porch where the dog was napping. The dog, suddenly aroused from slumber, may have jumped into the path of the customer. Whatever the cause, there was a collision between the man and the dog. Mr. Hinckley was standing near the door and he swore that the man kicked his dog. Hot words were exchanged and the customer declared that he would never again speak to the dog's owner. He never did. But he continued to trade at the store, taking pains to make his purchases from Mr. Merrill. The dog lived a long life and continued to bear witness against the short-tempered native. Whenever the man entered the store, the dog sought shelter behind the counter.

My Aunt Fannie Maddocks had pleasant memories of Mr. Hinckley. When Grandfather Maddocks went to Merrill and Hinckley's to do his trading, she was his glad companion. I use the word trading with accuracy. Grandfather took eggs and butter to the store. Mr. Hinckley wrote in the back of the Maddocks' storebook the date of the transaction, the amount of the produce and the price. When Grandfather paid his bill at the end of the month, he was given credit for the value of the articles that he had brought in. Settling the monthly account, a matter of some ceremony, was climaxed by the presentation of a small gift to little Fannie. Usually the gift was a stick of candy or a box of cracker-jack. But one memorable Saturday, when the grocer was rejoicing over the birth of a third son, he went to the china shelf and took from it a match holder in the form of a lady with a full shirt and becurled hair-do. He placed the holder in the child's hands. My aunt was too delighted to say thank you, even though her father urged her to speak.

After the deaths of Mr. Merrill and Mr. Hinckley the two sons of the latter ran the store. They were called by their first names. Perhaps they lived in less formal times. Perhaps the villagers felt that the sons should not be given the title so long bestowed upon their father. In my Academy days I became well acquainted with the Hinckley brothers. We girls considered that Gale was handsome, very handsome indeed. When we bought candy or cookies or punch for a social or a class picnic, we liked to make our purchase from Gale but we preferred to pay the bill to Max, the older of the brothers. He would carefully add up the figures, taking pains that there was no error and then he would ask, "How much did you make at the social?" After he had carefully listened to our accounting of profits, he tore up the bill, always making the same remark, "Since I was unable to go to the social, I would like to make a little contribution."

As the years went by, Max became famous for his "little contributions" to school socials, lodge suppers and church teas. On winter afternoons when the schoolchildren flocked into the store he was quick to notice when the son or daughter of a poor family needed a jacket or overshoes. He had a way of signaling "come back when you are alone." When the child returned alone, Max gave him a new jacket or overshoes.

One day when I was quite a young lady and was shopping at Merrill and Hinckley's, a group of children gathered around a table where there was a display of china. A little girl picked up a cup to admire it. The cup slipped from her fingers, falling on other cups and breaking them. The child burst into tears; the other children ran from the store, and a clerk rushed up to scold the girl. His scolding was cut short by Max who bade him, "Go back to your work. I'll attend to this." He picked up the child, sat her on the counter, wiped away her tears and said, "Let me tell you, you have done me a favor. I never had such ugly china. No one will ever buy it. Let's pick up the saucers and the three cups that are left and go behind the store and break them on a rock."

Jerry, the third generation Hinckley to own the store, carried on the traditions of his grandfather, uncle, and father. The Academy young people always knew where to find a listener to their problems and a financier for their projects.

I am glad that the present owner of the old village store keeps the name of Merrill and Hinckley. I am glad that I own the match holder, a reminder of men who knew that good storekeeping is more than just selling goods.

the owen family

The Owen Family was among the summer people who came to Blue Hill early in the twentieth century. There were three sisters and a brother, all unmarried, though there was a rumor that Brother David had once had a wife. The sisters were Elizabeth, Mary, and Caroline but they were always called Sister Bessie, Sister Minnie, and Sister Carrie. Carrie was the youngest; she had a bad back and was an invalid. Rumor had it that one of her older sisters had dropped her when she was a baby. The father of the family had been a Union general in the Civil War and had fought at the second Battle of Bull Run. The older sisters owned and operated a tea shop called the Green Dragon in their home city of Philadelphia. Brother David had no visible means of support, but he was kept busy following his sisters directions.

Their summer home was built on a seaboard cliff between Friend's Corner and the Head-of-the-Bay. They lived in some style, with a chauffeur, cook, and waitress, all "native help." I use an expression of half a century ago. No native regarded himself as a servant and resented the use of the term.

After a time the Owens had a second cottage. They bought the old office of a nearby granite company, enlarged it, painted it pink, and called it Larkspur Lodge. Then they opened a tea shop there. Sister Minnie presided over the tea arrangements and Sister Bessie sold gifts imported from Europe and the Orient. Sister Carrie was too frail to do anything other than arrange the bouquets for the tea tables. Brother David daily raked the road between Larkspur Lodge and the big cottage, Teeni Koad. (The last is a Welsh name. I have never seen the name in writing and I am sure that my spelling will offend anyone of Welsh origin.)

Brother David was a short, broad-shouldered man. His face was round and red, his teeth very white, his eyes sharp and bright. He liked to tell stories. When he finished a story, he always said, "I have to laugh." And then he laughed. He sang tenor in the choir of the Congregational Church. To again quote rumor, he at one time was an opera singer. Our summer people came from Cleveland, Chicago, Baltimore, Washington, Philadelphia, East Orange and Boston. Local rumor was kept busy getting together the odds and ends of their lives.

The sisters, rather short women with long brown hair, dressed beautifully; each had a color for her wardrobe. Miss Bessie's was green; Miss Minnie's, blue; Miss Carrie's, purple. The shades of blue, green and purple differed from light to dark. A dress might be flowered; a coat might be trimmed with a black velvet collar, but never did a sister forget herself and use the color of another.

Once when I was a very small child, I went on a picnic given by the Curtis Family. I was the guest of little Janie Curtis. The guests of honor were Brother David and his sisters. Janie and I went early with her parents to the picnic site on the shore. The cloth was spread on a flat rock, the picnic baskets unpacked, and potatoes were baking in the coals of the driftwood fire when the Owenses arrived. Their chauffeur drove them in the car to the spot where a rail fence closed the meadow road. There they got out of the car and walked the few rods down the sloping field to the shore. Brother David came first, swinging his cane and beheading buttercups and daisies. He shouted, "I've a story I have to tell you." Next came the sisters. Miss Bessie wore a green linen dress; Miss Minnie, a blue one; Miss Carrie, a purple one. Each shaded her head with a parasol that matched her gown. The chauffeur brought up the rear. He carried three cushions: a green one for Miss Bessie, a blue one for Miss Minnie, a purple one for Miss Carrie.

I have pleasant memories of the jovial David and his friendly sisters. But I also have sad memories. Miss Carrie was the first to die. She was buried in a sunken garden on the estate. After their brother died, the law journal in which the family means were invested failed, the Green Dragon was closed and the older sisters were in straightened circumstances. But they continued to live in genteel style and to keep the family color code.

In the early part of this century, when the summer people and the natives were strangers to each other, the summer people told stories about the natives and the natives told stories about the summer people. Some of these stories are worth retelling.

The musician Franz Kneisel was one of the town's favorite part-time residents. There was good fellowship between him and any man who worked for him. They laughed at each other and they laughed together.

One day when Mr. Kneisel was playing classical music on his violin, he noticed that his workman Fred was clipping grass under the window. When he finished playing, he went to the open window and asked, "How did you like my playing?" Came back the quick answer, "Pretty good, Mr. Kneisel, but you ought to hear my friend play 'The Turkey in the Straw.' "

Another time Mr. Kneisel noticed Fred on the lawn and it seemed to him that Fred was doing little work. So he stepped to the window and this conversation followed:

"Fred, what are you doing?"

"Helping, helping Rufus."

"What is Rufus doing?"

"Nothing."

In my childhood "helping Rufus" became a local expression meaning doing nothing.

One of Mr. Kneisel's neighbors was a lady from the midwest who was spending her first summer on the coast. One August day she decided to have her boatman row her to the village for the mail. "Frank," she said to the man, "leave off painting the steps and row me to the village."

"But Madam," said Frank, "the tide is way out."

Answered the lady, "I don't care where the tide is. I own the boat. You work for me. When I say we are going to the village, we are going."

"Very well," agreed Frank as he cleaned the paint brush.

The two got into the rowboat. With rapid strokes Frank rowed the boat away from Parker Point, to the inner bay, by the Sand Island and into the village harbor. It was a harbor without water. Frank rowed as far as he could and then beached the boat in the mud. Rods of mud separated the boat from the shore.

The woman rose to the occasion. She said, "Frank, turn your back to me for a minute."

In a moment she said, "You may turn around."

She had removed her shoes and her stockings, stepped from the boat, and with skirt and petticoat folded back over her arm, she was prepared to walk to shore. She said, "You may row home. I'll get a ride home with the Kneisels who drove to the village for their mail."

The incident taught both the lady and the man. She learned about the tide and the wisdom of taking local advice. He learned that his employer, out-of-towner though she was, had grit and a sense of humor.

In 1907, when Mr. Brooks bought land at Friend's Corner and built his bungalow, he was overwhelmed with the pride of ownership. He had been a poor boy; he had always been a city man. He loved to walk about his property and talk of "my shore" and "my field" and "my woods" and "my brook."

One late July afternoon when the mackerel were running, a motorboat ran into the cove below the Brooks field and men started to fish. The indignant Mr. Brooks seized his bull's horn, hurried to the back veranda and shouted to the fishermen, "What are you doing? I don't want you on my property. Go away!"

The fishermen, too, had a bull's horn. One of them shouted back to Mr. Brooks. What he shouted had best remain unrecorded.

The next day my father explained to Mr. Brooks that land ownership extended only to the reach of the high tide. The new land owner was surprised and ashamed. "I'm an outlander here," he said, "I can see that I have a lot to learn. By Jingo! I ought to apologize to those chaps."

My father replied, "Forget about the apology. Just remember that we natives do not like to be shouted at—especially through a bull's horn."

Mr. Brooks smiled when he said, "And you might well add, 'especially when the shouter is a fool, a greenhorn, and a stranger.' "

Father knew just what to say, "Mr. Brooks, you are no fool. After a few summers of living in the country you will no longer be a greenhorn. You are not a stranger—you are my neighbor."

Now that we natives and the summer people are neighbors rather than strangers, we tell fewer stories about each other.

walking in style

The summer people in our neighborhood during the years of my childhood enjoyed walking. They walked with style. The men carried canes. A walker swinging a cane labeled himself as "being from away." I noticed that none of them sought support from their canes. Mr. Loring aimed his at the roadside wild flowers and cut down the blossoms as though he swung a sythe. Mr. Owen used his to push the stones from his gravel driveway. Mr. Curtis's cane got hard use. He wet it when he skimmed the leaves from the teahouse spring; he bent it when he used it as a culvert cleaner. He was known to use it as an ox goad when he teamed the oxen, as a weapon when he killed snakes.

Our near neighbor, Mr. Brooks, had the greatest number of canes though he was not a great walker. He had a cane for his own special use marked with a silver plate bearing the initials *E.J.B.* He had a cane for "Mama," one for son Win, one for daughter Elinor, one for his sister-in-law, several for his brothers-in-law, and a bevy of slender sticks for the young people who visited the family. Two umbrella stands held the canes: metal canes, wooden canes, bamboo canes, canes with handles and canes with no handles, canes with curved handles and canes with square-cornered handles.

When I was a very small child I once went with Father when he called on Mr. Brooks. Mr. Brooks invited Father to sit by the fireplace. He had a happy inspiration for my entertainment. "Little Esther," he said, "I'll take all these canes to the front porch and you may play with them."

Once the canes and I were alone, I "played tea party" with them and placed each cane across the arms of a chair. There was no doubt as to which cane was Mr. Brooks. I chose a stout cane with a pearl handle for Mrs. Brooks.

Mr. Brooks once used his cane as a weapon. He was proud of the granite trough he had installed on a roadside corner near his property. It was meant for the horses but Professor Pender's red setter did not understand this provision. Every weekday the Penders drove in their red Dart to the Head-of-the-Bay for their mail. The dog followed them. The dog was always tired and dust covered by the time they reached the Corner. Into the water-filled trough he dove.

Mr. Brooks phoned Professor Pender; he wrote notes to him. The reply was always the same: "The spring is on town land. My dog has as much right to use it as do your neighbors' horses."

Mr. Brooks decided that direct action was needed. One warm Thursday in August he hid behind a clump of bushes near the spring at the time when the Penders usually drove by. He carried his cane under his arm. That morning Mrs. Pender had chosen to pause at Mrs. Lawson's to buy some eggs. Therefore, the dog arrived at the Friend's Corner neighborhood first. As usual he rushed to the trough for his cooling plunge. Out rushed Mr. Brooks shaking his cane and shouting like a madman. The dog was no fighter; he turntailed, ran, and with loud yelps of terror, met his folks at the top of the Corner hill.

Mr. Brooks was standing in front of the trough when the car jerked to a halt. "Sir," shouted the professor, "I accuse you of frightening my dog."

Mr. Brooks smiled and remarked, "You may accuse all you like, Professor. Neither the dog nor I will testify."

The dog could not testify by speech but he did testify by his actions. Never again did he bathe in the Corner spring.

I do not recall that the "summer ladies" were cane users. They did, however, walk with their husbands. Mrs. Mary Curtis always carried a book. When she tired of walking, she sat on a roadside boulder and read until her Ben came back from his "constitutional." Mrs. Josie Brooks always carried an open parasol to protect her face from the sun. Mrs. Rachel Gale carried nothing when she started on a walk. When she returned, she had wild flowers, a profusion of them, swung over her left shoulder and steadied with her right hand. Mrs. Gale was still young and beautiful. I believe that she enjoyed making a picture. The bouquet she carried always complemented her gown. I still recall the shoulder-load of goldenrod that complemented her purple suit.

Walking summer people presented an awesome sight to timid native children. My Aunt Fannie, a little child in the first decade of this century, told me that when she was on the road and saw a cane-swinging figure approaching, she ran into the woods and hid behind a tree until the walker had gone from sight. Mary Ellen Chase used to tell of her childhood task of driving the cow to the pasture in the morning and driving her back in the late afternoon. The post-breakfast walk presented no problems: the cow was eager to get to the pasture and the summer folks were not afoot so early. But in the afternoon Mary was sure to meet people out for their walks. The sight of strangers made the cow shy and threaten to run. It was worse when the strangers stopped Mary and her charge. They asked, "Do you milk the cow?" "How much milk does the cow give?" "How old are you?" Then Mary would wish that both she and the cow could run back to the pasture.

When Mary grew up and became a college teacher and a writer, she returned to her hometown summers. Twice a day, she went to walk. She enjoyed walking; she walked with style; she carried a cane.

The coming of the "summer people" to eastern Maine is a topic that has been well explored by novelists and article writers. Their sailboats, their cottages and their Stanley Steamers have been described. Their plush hotels and clubs and music centers have had their share of publicity. But those who waited on them have had little attention.

In the early decade of the twentieth century most of the city folks who summered in Blue Hill brought three servants with them: a cook, a waitress, and a chambermaid. Their employers called a waitress "the second girl"; the chambermaid "the third girl." The cook ranked first but, oddly enough, she was never called "the first girl." Blue Hillers spoke of the servants as "the help." Usually the servants from the city were Irish or Scandinavian. Now and then there was an Italian or black worker.

I have warm recollections of some of those who worked in the homes of our rich neighbors.

The was Mary, an Italian nursemaid who cared for little Janey Curtis. When Jane grew too old to have a nursemaid, Mary stayed on as the cook and family friend. I was Jane's playmate so I knew Mary's love and care, and, on occasion, her correction. In time, Mary wed. Forty years later she came back to the Corner, an old woman, gray-haired and bent. She came to our door and asked, "Do the Woods still live here? Of course there would be no one who would know me." When I interrupted her to say, "I know you. You are Mary Morelli," she burst into tears. My eyes were wet too.

There was Rachel, who cooked for the Walkers of Canadian whiskey fame. Rachel was the queen of the kitchen. She ordered the supplies; she planned the meals and she cooked them. She was a motherly lady in her fifties who loved to see people eat. One summer she enjoyed feeding Oscar, a teen-ager who mowed the lawns in the neighborhood. One late August day, Mrs. Walker came to the kitchen to interview Rachel. She said, "I am not complaining, but I do wish to ask a question: why do we have coffee cream pie twice a week?"

Rachel answered, "There is reason enough. Coffee pie is what Oscar likes best."

Two retired schoolteachers were our summer neighbors for over thirty years. One summer they had a cook who had worked for the Maryland Dobbins family for over forty years. After the death of the mother and the three daughters, she had consented to spend a summer cooking for the teachers, who were old friends of the youngest Miss Dobbins. The cook from Maryland made delicious beaten biscuits. Her roasts were brown and savory; her vegetables were delicately flavored.

But a problem arose over desserts. The teachers liked them rich and luscious. When they asked for a three-layer cake they were told, "I'll make you one like I always made the Dobbinses—two layers, sprinkled with powdered sugar." When they suggested a lemon pie the former Dobbins cook remarked, "The Miss Dobbinses didn't like lemon pie. I'll make you lemon Jell-o." The teachers soon learned that the Dobbins family had not eaten cream puffs or fudge cake or berry pie or jelly roll or any number of desserts usually made in their Maine kitchen. During the summer the Maryland cook was resident in their kitchen, the teachers ate only the desserts that "Miss Dobbinses ate."

Mrs. Brooks, one of our favorite neighbors, preferred help from Sweden. For two summers she had the beautiful blonde, pink-cheeked Julia as a waitress. Mr. Brooks used to say, "When Julia serves a meal, she is the most beautiful woman in the room." He could have added, "And the most cultured." She spoke German and French as well as she spoke English and Swedish. When invited, she played classical music on the Brooks' piano. Her trunk was half filled with books.

After being with the Brooks family for two years, Julia went home to Sweden. She and Mrs. Brooks wrote to each other. After Mrs. Brooks died her daughter Elinor continued the correspondence. In time Elinor went to Europe and was invited to visit Julia, who had been married for a decade. Julia and her husband met Elinor at the station and drove her to their country estate where there were gatekeepers, gardeners, governesses, nursemaids, a housekeeper, a butler, and many housemaids. Elinor was more than a little surprised and she said to the onetime waitress, "Julia, why did you not write me that you had married so well?"

Julia's reply showed that she had a tender humility that matched her beauty and culture: "Why should I have written you? I am the same Julia who served you at your dear mother's dinner table. God rest her soul."

Maine people still work in the homes of our "summer people." Often a happy and affectionate relationship develops. With the passing years, the employer leans more heavily on the judgement and ministrations of the employee. Local men spend a lifetime as gardeners or caretakers or boatmen in the employment of the same family. Long association results in the growth of firm friendships between those who live in cottages and those who live in clapboard houses.

rusticators and cottagers

In 1908 Mrs. Vergil Kline wrote a paper about the Blue Hill summer colony. She recorded that the first summer boarder was Mrs. Emma Drummond Dole from Bangor who came to town in the summer of 1884. I have been thinking about Mrs. Dole. How did she happen to come to Blue Hill? Why did her husband not come with her? How did she travel? Perhaps she came to Bucksport by the Bangor boat or to Ellsworth by train. Whether she started her journey by boat or by train, she must have ended it in a horse-drawn vehicle.

I believe I know where she stayed. Likely she boarded with Mr. and Mrs. Hartford Sweet who in 1879 had moved from Salem to Blue Hill where they bought Parker Point from Israel Parker. They took summer boarders and soon gave an acre of land to two star boarders, Mr. and Mrs. Rogers, who built the first summer house on the Point. Mr. George Butler was the builder.

In later years boarders might have stayed at the Snow House, the Blue Hill House, the Pendleton House, or Blue Hill Inn. The Inn atop Tenney Hill had wide verandas that gave a fine view of both the bay and the mountain. It sought to imitate the stylish hotels of Bar Harbor and Newport. The inn closed about 1908 and became the home of the Truax Family. Some people chose to board in private homes. Mr. and Mrs. R.G.W. Dodge in the Village and Captain and Mrs. Ralph Long in East Blue Hill opened their homes to boarders.

During my childhood in the second decade of this century, the term summer boarder had gone out of use. We spoke of the "rusticators" and the "cottagers." All those who came to town to spend a few weeks of leisure were called rusticators or 'cators. The people who lived in their own dwellings and walked to the Inn or Sweet's for meals were called cottagers. The Curries and the Rousseaus were first summer boarders, then they bought farmhouses near the Inn and became cottagers; finally they ate at home and were called summer people. I have heard Mrs. Rousseau laugh about the conflict when one of her little boys insisted on taking his doll with him when the family went to the Inn for dinner. Admiral Rousseau was firm that no son of his should be seen in the company of a doll. The doll battle was one that the Admiral lost.

The number of summer people who owned their own homes increased after 1886. Hill and Holman bought twenty acres of the Point from the Sweets. They laid out lots, surveyed roads, built bathing houses and sold land. They had a wharf constructed on the end of the Point so that the steamer *Henry Morrison* could call at the Point with passengers from Rockland who had come from Boston, New York, Chicago and Washington. Mrs. Kline wrote that by 1908 twenty-three cottages had been built in the vicinity of Parker Point, six summer people resided in the Village, two summer families on South Street, four such families in East Blue Hill. Mrs. Kline used the term summer people loosely. Three of her summer families were native families who wintered out of town.

In 1893, Mr. Wolf Fries, the musician, came to Blue Hill. Other musicians followed him. Mr. Franz Kneisel, Horatio Parker, Mr. Krehbiel and Mr. Willike made the town a music center. Later Mr. Bostleman and the talented Dethier Family came to East Blue Hill. These musicians brought another type of summer people—the roomers. There were young students who slept and practiced their violins in private homes and ate their meals in boarding houses or inns.

Some of the newcomers bought village homes or country farmhouses. Most gave their homes loving care; others "improved" them out of all recognition by adding turrets and towers and verandas. Others chose to build new structures, many of them out of place in a country town. There were an Italian villa, a French chateau, and numerous bungalows. The Slaven cottage, partially built of local granite and modeled after a Dutch homestead, fitted into its surroundings. Mr. Ward Hinckley built a beautiful home, a small-scale version of a Frank Lloyd Wright house. Mr. Wallace Hinckley was the builder.

The home of a summer person, whether it was large or small, whether it was palatial or modest, was called a cottage. Most of them were given a name. Mrs. Kline called her home, a farmhouse-turned-castle, "Ideal Lodge."

The early summer residents of Blue Hill were enthusiastic, to say the least, about their summer town. I quote high words of praise published in the Ellsworth American at the close of the nineteenth century:

> *The sunsets from Caterpillar Hill are a feature of the joys of the summer population of Blue Hill, a population which is largely musical and therefore aesthetically sensitive, and which has surrounded itself with a world of exquisite beauty. The whole of Blue Hill is pure country—save for the idle and jungle-grown copper mines buildings. The walks about Blue Hill are most alluring. Never a place of more spontaneous delights for body and spirit than Blue Hill.*

Now we have many summer residents in Blue Hill. Some of them have been coming to town for over fifty years. Many of them are great-grandchildren of the rusticators of the last century. Some of them are newcomers. The term summer person is going out of use just as did the terms of summer boarder and cottager and rusticator. I am glad that this is so. I believe that all who live in Blue Hill should be called "Blue Hillers."

Country Ways

sea language ashore

Sea language came ashore in Maine in the seventeenth, eighteenth, and nineteenth centuries. Few Maine men can today tell the difference between a brig and a brigantine. None sail square-riggers around Horn or take schooner voyages to the Carribean. But still the people of coastal Maine use the nautical terms of their seafaring forebears. Down East speech is richer because of this salty inheritance. Joanna C. Colcord's *Sea Language Comes Ashore* lists over one thousand words of nautical origin that are used alongshore in Maine.

My Searsport friend and I use sea language. We do not choose to use it; it comes to our tongues naturally, and well it should. Her grandfather captained China ships—mine, Caribbean schooners. She and I understand each other perfectly. When I say, "I am going to have clam chowder for supper," she knows that I shall eat a mixture of clams, potatoes, milk, and salt pork, uncontaminated by peas and tomatoes. When she tells me that she had lobscouse or slumgullion for dinner, she does not need to define them as hash and beef stew.

When I tell her that a lost sweater was found in the glory hole, she knows that I refer to the closet under the front stairs. Aboard ship the glory hole held valuables but ashore it has come to mean a cluttered storage area. When I mention my ditty bag, she knows that I am talking about my sewing box. A sailor's ditty bag was made of canvas and held odds and ends.

She and I share a common weather vocabulary: smur up (to become cloudy or overcast); thick (air filled with snow or driving rain); to herm up (sky showing signs of bad weather); to burn off (disappearance of fog or mist in the sun); wind backing in (wind going from east to north to west). Mackerel skies and mares' tails and sea glins are all expressions that please us.

One night last winter when my friend and I left the home of a mutual friend who lives outside the village, we discovered that the driving conditions were bad.

"Thick-a-fog," Miss Searsport remarked.

"Regular pea souper," I replied. "You'll never be able to get your bearings."

"Oh, yes I shall," she countered, "Just roll down your window and pilot me."

When we neared a stop sign at the crossroads, I called out, "Ease up, ease up." When she drove near a bridge railing, I shouted, "Shear off, shear off." And when we at last saw the lights of the village through the fog, we both exclaimed, "Home, ahoy."

When we are with another friend who was born and raised in New Hampshire, we avoid using our sea lingo. She does not understand saltwater expressions and quite naturally laughs at them. One day last spring I forgot myself and referred to a self-made young man as "coming in through the hawsehole." The hawsehole is the opening through which the anchor chain passes, so the term is used to describe a captain who has worked his way up from the galley to the forecastle. The lady from the White Mountains laughed and laughed. After a time, I explained what the expression means. Then she said, "You two granddaughters of sea captains should be boxed up and sent to a marine museum." And she laughed some more.

Storytelling

Maine country people have been telling stories ever since David Ingram walked from Florida to Maine in the late sixteenth century. Ingram, a sailor afoot looking for an England-bound ship, told tall tales about Maine, then called Northern Virginia. He reported that the savages had pearls and great nuggets of gold and that there was a rich inland city. His stories were believed in England as were the tales of his successors, Pring and Weymouth and John Smith.

Maine people have followed the practice of their colonial predecessors in seasoning their stories with imagination. They tell of the farmer who shingled his barn roof in a fog mull and nailed three feet of shingles on the fog; of the woman who got a fresh cod for dinner by knocking down with her broom a fish-carrying gull; of the boy who shot the oversized clams before he dug them.

The weather is always a favorite topic for storytellers. They recall stories of "eighteen-hundred-and-froze-to-death"—1816—when there was a frost every month of the year. The great *Portland* storm of 1898 that took a heavy toll on Maine shipping is remembered every November when folks recall how a grandfather or an uncle or a neighbor nearly went on the *Portland* for her last fatal trip out of Boston. Winters of severe cold and deep snow, springs of flood, summers of drought, and autumns of fire are all remembered.

In coastal towns captains are always heroes of stories. Captain Oscar Crockett, who piloted the Eastern Steamship Company steamers out of Rockland in the early decades of this century, was one such hero. All the stories about him pointed up his skill and his mental keenness. One day an admiring passenger said to him, "Oh, Captain Crockett, I expect you know where every rock in this bay is." The Captain shot back the answer, "No, Ma'am, but I do know where there are no rocks."

Blue Hill's last deep-water captain was John Warren Kane, a man who was contemptuous of conceit. One day in a local store he was the unseen hearer of a young man's proud account of his distant travels. When the youth finished his account, Captain Kane stepped out of the store's office and exclaimed, "Travels, travels, why boy, you have not been anywhere but I'd just as soon go there in my flunkett with one oar."

A landlubber's failure to understand sea language is the theme of many Maine yarns. One such story tells of a captain who took a farm boy on a coasting trip with him. When they neared the wharf where they were to unload a cargo of kiln wood, the captain said, "Let go the anchor."

There was no move from his young helper.

Then the captain shouted, "Boy, let go that anchor at once."

The annoyed boy replied in kind and shouted, "Stop yelling at me. I'm not touching your darned old anchor." The captain's answer was drowned by the crash when the schooner piled up on the wharf.

One of my father's favorite stories was about a prosperous Hancock County farmer who in the days of Prohibition was suspected of selling liquor that he brought in from Canada. One June day the sheriff and a deputy appeared at the farm with a search warrant.

The farmer met them at the back door. At his side was his little granddaughter; in front of him were two hounds; on the step were two cats; in the barrel at the foot of the step was a mother cat with a litter of kittens. The farmer was most cordial. He said, "Look anywhere you like, upstairs or downstairs or in the lady's chamber. The little girl is my granddaughter; she never has much to say. Her name is Daisy; the hounds are Surprise and Silence; the cats are

Pete, Jo, and Nan. We have not yet named the kittens. While you make yourself at home, I'll go back to my accounts."

The sheriff hitched his horse to the hitching post. He and his deputy made the rounds of the barns, the grain room, the henhouse, the carriage house, the cellar, and the house. Daisy was a grave and silent companion. Finally they gave up; they unhitched their horse; they got into the buggy. The farmer came out of the house to bid them farewell and took little Daisy by the hand. When the sheriff picked up the reins, Daisy broke her silence, "Mr. Men, you forgot to look in the kitty's barrel."

They looked.

They found five dozen bottles of whiskey, Canada's best.

Writing letters

Country women are usually letter writers. They agree with the essayist who wrote, "Letters are comforters and they are also heart-talkers."

I read and reread a letter from a friend. I miss the voice of an absent friend but her written words give me companionship. Spoken words are sometimes misunderstood but written ones are seldom misinterpreted. Emerson said it better than I can:

The tongue is prone to lose the way;
Not so the pen for in a letter
We have not better things to say
But surely say them better.

Country people cherish letters. A Rockland cousin recently found letters that had been saved for eighty years. My Newfield friend has the 1850 correspondence of her great-grandfather and great-grandmother. My mother saved the tri-weekly letters I wrote to her. I must confess that I save letters too. My scrapbooks are filled with them.

Three of my former correspondents were women thirty or forty years older than I. They are no longer living. The first was Mrs. Hattie Bisset, the friend and contemporary of my mother. Though she had brothers and sisters, children and grandchildren to whom she wrote, she found time to write to me. She wrote regularly over a period of twenty-five years. I regret that I saved none of her letters. But I remember them and recall her rounded script. She wrote about the town, her family, and her home chores. She wrote in such a personal way that she took me shopping with her; she sat a place at the table for me; she handed me the dish towel.

The second correspondent was Cousin Ethel Howard. I have a number of her letters and have just reread them. Some letters were written to answer questions that I had asked about her childhood at the Corner. Others she wrote to tell of her life in California. But whether she wrote about a country fair or the Golden Gate Exposition, she expressed her own joy in living. Perhaps her joy was the elixir that gave her more than the Biblical three-score and ten.

The third was my Great-Aunt Fan. She made a business of letter writing and to her it was a delightful business. She wrote at the big desk between the kitchen windows. The many drawers of the desk were filled with letters—ones that she had answered. Every few years she sorted them and took them to the ell chamber. Her unanswered letters were kept on a box atop the desk. There were never many letters in the box because Aunt answered her letters promptly. She devoted the afternoons of Saturday and Sunday to her correspondence. Her letters were epistles, extensive in length and cosmopolitan in tone. She treated her cats and her Congressmen with equal familiarity. Famine in China and the smelt-run in Peter's Brook shared the same page. No celebrity, no international policy, and no presidential pronouncement was above her comment and criticism.

I have one of Aunt Fan's letters. It was written to me when I was a freshman at Colby College. She laughed at me for finding fault with the dormitory meals and wrote that she had cold beans for lunch. She described her battle with the outside windows and reported the casualty of a pounded thumb. Her narrative of the state of the neighborhood sparkled with humor. She referred to Uncle Frank's scholastic honors. The tone of her letter was clear: any niece of hers should have fewer thoughts of food and more about lessons.

Aunt Fan's Christmas writing was impressive. She wrote long letters to distant cousins and to old friends who had once lived in Maine. In return she expected letters from them. She expressed her wrath when her letters were not answered. Some of her relatives and friends disappointed her, but not Lottie Morton of Chicago. I recall Miss (or was it Mrs.?) Morton's letters, sheet after sheet, every one unnumbered. Aunt delighted to receive such a letter and she was more delighted to answer it.

I am a country woman. I like to write letters. My letters do not have the warmth of Hattie Bisset's. They are not as joyous as Cousin Ethel's. They are not as long or as cosmopolitan as were Aunt Fan's. But I shall continue to write letters. I know that my friends have enough imagination to understand and appreciate what I am trying to say.

Keeping a diary

Keeping a diary is a good Maine custom. Some were kept on the margins of the *Old Farmer's Almanac*; others were scribbled on the back of the leaves of the calendar. A home long owned by the same family is sure to have in its attic an old trunk filled with diaries.

There have been three lifelong diarists in my family. Cousin Henry wrote a diary for over sixty years, recording his daily entries in a small lined book that he kept in his vest pocket. His old diaries were stored in a discarded desk in the attic where they were ready for instant research when someone might inquire about the date of the *Portland* gale or the weather on the day of the first Armistice.

Great-aunt Mary wrote the record of the daily events on her Dedham homestead and her reactions to state and national events on a lined tablet. I have some of her diaries but I cannot read them because it was Great-aunt's thrifty habit to use a sheet twice, first writing the length of the sheet and then the width. Sometimes I look over her diaries and find that nouns appear in strange and nonsensical conjunction. A page for April 8, 1912 especially intrigues me because I find the names of President Taft and Senator Hale and the words, tea, jelly-roll, and porcupine. I am sure that Great-aunt never had the President for tea but it is conceivable that the Senator might have dropped in at teatime. Was he served jelly-roll? Did a porcupine break up the tea party? I shall never know.

Mother's diaries, dating back four decades and more, were kept in little bound volumes which have some twenty lines for each day. Her records, in beautifully legible script, deal with wind and weather, with war and politics, with gardens and kitchens, with family joys and sorrows. I frequently read the books with mingled feelings of gladness and sorrow.

However, my favorite diarist is the Reverend Thomas Smith, the first minister of Falmouth (now Portland). Mr. Smith kept a journal from 1722 to 1787, years that brought threat of fire and famine, wars with the French, deadly Indian attacks, and finally revolution to the saltwater frontier settlement.

Thomas Smith, a Harvard graduate, came to Falmouth as a young man and he died there at the age of ninety-three. There he was thrice married and there he brought up eight children, only two of whom survived him. He doctored the bodies of his parishioners as well as ministering to their souls. He had a garden and an orchard. He went to outlying settlements to preach. When councils of war or peace were called, he was among the councilmen.

"Things are in a sad toss," was a favorite expression when he wrote about parish quarrels, Indian attacks, and severe droughts. "War, what havoc dost thou make," started his narrative of an attack by the French and the Indians.

In spite of vexations and sorrows, Thomas Smith was a man who loved life. It pleased him to dine with the governor and to be the friend of Colonel Waldo and Colonel Westbrook and other leaders of the time. He liked fun and laughter. One surprising entry tells of a postordination meeting in which the ministers enjoyed hearty laughter.

The Parson always rejoiced over the "beautiful green face of the earth," "beautious showers," and the "flowering of my heart cherry trees." I am sure that spring was his favorite season because the sentences that he used to describe it read almost like a psalm of happiness: "April comes in smiling . . . The robin and the spring birds begin to tune up . . . A wonderful smile of providence is in the snow going away."

The lover of singing birds and flowering trees was no great admirer of winter, as his terse entries prove: "Lion-like days . . . It is melancholy to see so much snow has fallen this late in March." I feel that he smiled when he wrote, "the snow goes away kindly."

Among my favorite Smith phrases are "peerless weather," "foul weather," "melancholy dry," "grievous drought," and "dreadful eastern weather." In December of 1750 he noted, "The year ends stingingly." When I go out in a severe rainstorm, I always quote the Falmouth preacher, "It has not rained so hard since the Flood."

Some of the minister's entries tell about eighteenth century traveling conditions: "Went to Falmouth on the ice"; "Incomparable sleighing." Falmouth of the Parson's day depended upon cutting trees for lumber and masts. It is to be expected that the depth of the snow in the woods concerned the Falmouth diarist.

Keeping a diary is a good Maine custom. I follow it. My entries about tide and wind and rain are not as meticulous as Cousin Henry's. I do not imitate Great-aunt Mary's twice-used page technique, nor is my writing beautiful like my mother's. But I do use Parson Smith's vocabulary. I write of "peerless days" and "nonesuch weather" and I rejoice in a "smiling Providence for an early melting of the snow."

There is not one native Maine accent. There are several. There are different pronunciations of surnames. In Hancock County we pronounce *Clough* to rime with the bow of a boat. We pronounce *Treworgy* as though it were *Trewergey*. When I started teaching in western Maine I found it hard to adjust to *Cluff* and *Treewergy*. Adjust I did, but I never accepted *Grindell* as the pronounciation of *Grindle*. I knew that Milford Grindle would turn over in his grave if his great-granddaughter corrupted his good English name.

Several first names have varied pronounciations in Maine. Two of my friends wanted to name their baby Sarah. The Blue Hill-born father pronounced the name *Sayrah*; the Springvale-raised mother said *Sara*. They decided to name the baby Susan.

Maine natives do not agree on the pronunciation of Bangor. Residents of Aroostook County say *Banger*. We coastal people say *Bang or*. The city on the Penobscot is a vexation to radio and TV announcers. They also have trouble with Saco and Machias. Actually *Sayco* sounds as good as *Socko*; *Makias* sounds as good as *Machiess*; but not to a Maine man's ear.

I once borrowed several books from the University library. One was a linguistic atlas and was likely the largest book ever delivered at the Blue Hill post office. The atlas contained many maps of New England showing how such familiar words as *mountain* and *family* and *cows* are pronounced differently in different sections. I read that there is a difference between "cultured speech" and "common speech." I learned that the coastal Maine speech has changed little because of our relative isolation and the dominance of those of English origin. I was reminded that coastal speech is seasoned with sea terms and enriched by such eighteenth century words as spider (frying pan), cricket (footstool), and crocus (coarse cloth).

I needed no reminder that there are words we coastal folks mispronounce: "loom" for loam, "ware" for weir, "hull" for whole, "yo" for ewe, "ketch" for catch, "hoss" for horse. I speak common coastal English. I admit that I prefer the sound of the corruption to the sound of the correct form.

I was surprised to read that we make excessive use of the preposition up: we dress up; we tare up; we fix up; we build up; we wake up; we wash up; we go up town. We use it as an prefix and talk of an upsweep, an updo and an upswing. When a proceeding appears to be prospering we say, "Things are on the up and up."

The editor of the atlas wrote that people of the Maine coast have trouble with the diphthong *ow* after a hard *c* or a *p*. He maintained that we sound an *e* or an *i* before the *ow*. I was indignant at the accusation. But in the case of *cow* and *power,* I am guilty as charged.

During my childhood Mrs. Bailey Bowden was the oldest resident at Friend's Corner. I noticed that she spoke some words in a strange way. I thought she was wrong and I felt ashamed for her. Now I know that she was using the eighteenth century pronunciation.

Now and then I talk of gathering "pineys" and "lilocs"; of picking "rozberries"; of using "cowcumbers" for pickling. After all, I am now the oldest resident of the Corner. Moreover, I'm in favor of keeping coastal Maine speech salty and distinctive.

lard pails

Lard pails were important to rural Maine housewives half a century ago. When the lard had been used for crumbly rich pastry, crusty brown doughnuts and crested white biscuits, the pails were washed in a soapy hot water and given a long airing in the sunshine.

A new lard pail became a dinner bucket for a child who took his noontime meal to the district school. The pupil who watched his mother pack the pail at the kitchen table with breakfast leftovers—biscuits, bacon, and doughnuts—knew the contents of the pail down to the last dill pickle. If the boy rushed for his lunch pail after he had slopped the calf and filled the woodbox, he lifted the cover to learn the contents of the pail on the way to school.

Besides a generous meal for a farm child, a well-packed pail provided items for swapping. By common agreement, a piece of frosted cake was worth two cookies or two doughnuts, while a slice of jelly-roll or a turnover was valued at three cookies or doughnuts. A cream puff was not for sale at any rate of exchange. Less fortunate pupils, condemned to a lard pail of soggy biscuits and fallen cake, often had scholastic information to barter for better cooking. The solution of an arithmetic problem was sometimes sold for a raspberry tart, and the answers to a geography question for a cupcake.

The contents of the dinner pails usually had been examined and partially exchanged by the time the pupils reached the schoolhouse. In warm weather the pails were lined up on the shady side of the building, and in winter were placed inside near the stove lest their contents freeze. At recess time a doughnut or cookie might be taken from a pail in spite of the parental warning, "Now don't nibble at your dinner during recess; it will only spoil your appetite."

But childhood appetites were never spoiled; when noontime came there was a glad rush for dinner pails and the noisy opening of the lids. In warm weather, the boys might retreat to the shed, while the girls gathered in the grove or the front yard. The teacher usually ate on the door rock but now and then she joined the girls and placed her lard pail among the others. In cold weather all the pupils were glad to huddle beside the woodstove while the teacher dined at her desk on the platform.

At the end of the school day the pails were given no preferential treatment on the walk home. In the fall, they were stained purple by the juice of the string cherries harvested by the wayside. In the spring, the children filled their pails with wild flowers and sometimes with pollywogs dipped from the pond. In the winter, the children used the pails as mallets to test the firmness of the ice in the pond and the ditches. And among the boys, when argument gave way to fisticuffs, the clash of lard pails rang louder than the angry words.

But rural children had no monopoly on lard pails. A good housewife always kept a few on a pantry shelf for special needs. When the hog was butchered in the fall, she tried out the grease and filled several pails with the homemade lard. A pail hanging in the cellarway was a handy receptacle for bringing vegetables up from the bins; it was just the right size for milk set to sour for pancakes and gingerbread mix. Now and then a child was handed a lard pail with the bidding, "Go down to Annie's and see if she'll lend me some sugar (or molasses or vinegar)."

A Maine farmer had dozens of uses for lard pails discarded by the housewife. Pails were hung from sap spouts on maple trees in spring. In the fall they were filled with seed corn and dried peas to make a festoon on the shed wall. A handleless pail became a water dish for the hens, or a seal to fill the gaping hole in the chimney after the removal of a stove pipe. Lard pails served a lethal purpose when they were filled with Paris green or rat poison, then tightly sealed and placed well back on a high shelf.

When farmers went into the woods to cut their supply of firewood, each carried an axe and two lard pails. One held the cutter's dinner—a rich fare of meat-filled bisuits and pie. The other was the tea pail which, near the noon hour, was hung over a brush fire from a forked stick. When the water in the pail boiled a generous handful of tea was added so that the men had a hot and potent drink for their dinner.

One Maine chopper insisted that he preferred cold tea to a hot brew. Every day he brought to the chopping a covered pail that he carefully set well away from the heat of the fire and the flurries of wood ashes. One day a thirsty friend took an unsuspecting swig from the pail and discovered that it held not cold tea, but cider, very cold and very old.

Calling round

"Paying a call" and "calling round" were two rural customs of my childhood that differed in purpose and practice.

Paying a call was a formal visit to a friend or acquaintance. Mother never paid such a visit without making careful plans and preparations. She selected a day when the morning tasks were less arduous than usual and when supper would be a meal easy to prepare. She arranged to have the use of the family team and she asked Cousin Austin to curry the horse and wash the buggy. Attired in her second best dress, wearing a hat, and taking her gloves in her bag, she drove out of the yard in style. Beside her on the seat there was always a basket; in spring and summer it held flowers; in fall and winter, jams and jellies—all designed as gifts for her village dwelling friends.

Calling round, which was occasioned by errand running, was a spur-of-the-moment chore that called for no preparation and no show of style on the part of the caller.

When Mother dug over her garden in the spring, resetting perennials, thinning out the volunteer annuals that had seeded themselves, and setting in the seedlings that had been raised in the kitchen and shed windows, she saved the surplus plants. She set clumps of phlox in the barnyard; she pushed pans of "volunteers" under the barn bench, and placed flats of surplus annuals on the shed walk. When Father complained that the plants were in the way, she always gave the same reply, "Tomorrow I plan to call round and give the plants away."

My Cousin Austin was drafted to fill the barrow with perennial roots, pans of volunteers, and flats of annuals. He pushed the barrow while Mother walked beside him with a trowel in her hand. They went from house to house in the neighborhood, leaving gifts for the garden. My cousin sometimes complained that the barrow was heavier when he returned home than when he left, because Mother could never turn down the gift of a plant. Pots of lilies, dahlia tubers, small shrubs, and tubs of geraniums were imported to the home garden, where somehow and somewhere room was found for them.

Mother's spring calling round did not always require the use of the barrow and the company of her nephew. With apron filled with asparagus or stalks of rhubarb (a country woman's favorite pie filling), she ran to a neighbor's in mid-morning. The first pulling of the early radishes, the first gathering of sweet peas, and the first picking of wild strawberries were all occasions for sharing with the neighbors and calling round.

Our Astrachan, the earliest bearing apple tree in the neighborhood, furnished fruit for August visiting. When my cousins and I brought home lard pails of fragrant raspberries and juice-filled blackberries, my mother called round with bowls of berries for our neighbors' suppers.

In the fall, when there were jars of jelly, pots of marmalade, and crocks of pickles to be shared with the neighbors, there was a daily ritual of calling round. In the autumn Father took up the habit, making the rounds of the neighborhood with pumpkins, squashes, and winter pears.

Sometimes Mother went empty-handed to the neighbors. It was then that she went to bring something home: a pattern from Cousin Ethel's, knitting needles from Annie's, and a spool of thread from Aunt Nellie's house.

Calling round meant both giving and receiving. It meant spending time for talk in a sunny kitchen cluttered with the tools of the forenoon's household tasks and fragrant with fresh baking. It was pleasant to see another woman at her cooking, to advise her about adding spice to her mincemeat, and to sympathize with her over a torn sheet or a broken dish.

When Mother was too busy to call round, I was always ready to leave swing or playhouse or storybook to take a gift to a neighbor or to borrow some article. I like to time my calling at mid-morning, an hour when Cousin Ethel was likely to be baking off cookies and Annie was likely to be watching doughnuts browning in a kettle of hot fat.

Calling round is an old rural custom that should be kept.

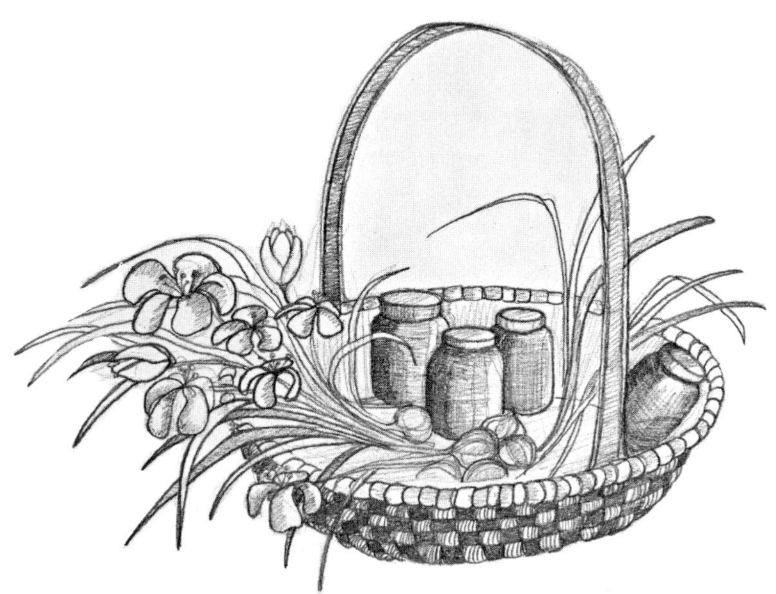

Country children of my generation repeated verses at their play.

Like our elders, we said verses that featured a sea glin, a red sky, clouds like towers, a rainbow, and mackerel skies. We had a variety of count-out verses for our games. I quote the opening lines of three: "Eenie, Meenie, Minie, Mo"; "Huckle-buckle, Huckle-eye"; "Engine, engine number nine, Going down Chicago line." We liked to pull apart a daisy and recite the familiar lines beginning, "Rich man, poor man." Sometimes we used the less familiar words, "One, I love; Two, he loves . . . Ten, they tarry; Eleven, they court; Twelve, they marry."

We greeted the evening with the wishing rhyme, "Star bright, star light," or with the verse beginning, "Twinkle, twinkle little star. How I wonder where where you are." When a shower displeased us we called out, "Rain, rain, go away. Come again some other day." Sometimes we would hold a grasshopper in our clasped hands and say, "Grasshopper, grasshopper, grasshopper gray, give me some molasses and I'll let you away." When a child's turn in the swing was over, he stopped pushing with his feet and his companions chanted, "Slow-lie, slow-lie, Let the old cat die."

When a post-April Fool prankster tried a joke, he was put in his place with the lines, "April Fool's Day has gone past, And you're the bigger fool at last." One April when we schoolchildren found Uncle Arthur in an apple tree cutting dead limbs, we rudely shouted, "Up a ladder, down a tree, You're a bigger fool than me." Uncle was not amused.

When Olive and I whistled, Harold or Austin was sure to call out, "Whistling girls and crowing hens always come to some bad ends." We knew what to shout back at them: "Whistling girls and Merino sheep are the very best crops for farmers to keep."

Some of our lines must certainly have been repeated by our fathers and grandfathers. I imagine that there is an overtone of nativism in them:

The old woman from Newfoundland
With all her children in her hand.

What's your name? Puddin-tame.
What's your number? Cucumber.

Fee, fi, fo, fum,
I smell the blood of an Englishmun.
Be he alive or be he dead,
I'll pound his bones to make me bread.

We repeated some verses which, in retrospect, seem highly inappropriate. Hancock County, Maine was a fortress of rock-ribbed Republicanism. (The bastion was finally weakened in 1912.) But we children delighted to say,

Ladies and gents,
Ladies and gents,
The Democratic Party
Is surely immense.

Abstinence was the rule of our elders; Prohibition was the law of the state, but my playmates and I knew and repeated the jolly lines,

Hey, down derry,
We'll drink and be merry
In spite of Neal Dow's law.

A river of whiskey,
If I were a duck,
I'd dive to the bottom,
And never come up.

We recited numerous long poems in unison. One gave the value of a hive of bees according to the month that the new swarm left the hive. It ended with the discouraging estimate: "But a swarm of bees in July is not worth a fly." Then there were the intriguing lines about a child's fate being determined by the day he was born. I felt discouraged that "Saturday's child works hard for a living," and I envied my cousins who, according to the verse, were fated to be "fair of face" or "full of grace."

Aunt Hannah Howard, whose childhood was in the 1850s, taught us poems that she had learned when she was a child. On occasion, the cousins repeated them to each other:

If half the time thus vainly spent
Were to heaven in supplication sent
Our cheerful song would oftener be
"See what the Lord hath done for me."

How pleasant is Saturday night
When we've tried all the week to be good,
When our actions were honest and right
And we've done all the work that we could.

It is not all in bringing up
Let folks say what they will.
Silver wash a pewter cup;
It will be pewter still.

It is not all in bringing up
Let folks say what they will.
Neglect may dim a silver cup;
It will be silver still.

smelting

Country people of the coastal towns like to catch smelts; they like to eat them, too.

Smelt tents are a familiar sight in eastern Maine. In the winter they are clustered on the ice of sheltered coves; in the summer they are huddled in saltwater meadows, waiting the return of the cold weather and the smelts. I have laughed many times at the comment of an up-country friend who exclaimed when we drove through Surry in August, "Look at all those doghouses in that field."

Maine natives behead the smelts, clean them, dip them in an egg batter, roll them in cornmeal and fry them in pork fat. No fish can rival the saltwater smelts in sweetness and flavor. Robert Peter Tristram Coffin once sang the praise of Casco Bay smelts and he recommended that they be fried "innards and all" and eaten "backbones and all."

Mr. Coffin failed to mention smelts-baked-in-a-beanpot. Grandmother used to produce this delectable dish every spring when the smelts were running well. She filled the old brown bean pot with the little fish, alternating the layers with brown sugar and filling the pot with a mixture of vinegar and water. The pot, left in the oven of the kitchen stove all day, furnished us with a supper fit for a king, especially when the fish dish was supplemented with buttermilk biscuits and spiced crab apples.

I ruefully admit that I have been smelting only twice. My smelting was not winter fishing, where the fisherman uses a line and hook thrown into the water through a hole in the ice beneath the sheltering smelt tent. My fishing was spring fishing, when we went to the brooks and dipped the fish from the water.

About thirty years ago I went smelting with my neighbors, the Dodges. We visited two brooks, the one at Morgan's Bay and the pasture brook at Friend's Corner. We saw only one smelt and he was floating belly up at the mouth of the brook. Though we caught no smelts, I still recall the curve of Long Island outlined against the sunrise and the fragrance of meadow lilacs wet with dew.

My second expedition was in my early childhood when I went with Great-aunt Emma to Little Peter's Brook which edged Grandfather Maddocks's farm. No villagers appeared to dip and so Aunt Emma and I and the smelts had the brook to ourselves. In those days smelting was not regulated. Great-aunt and I waded into the brook and soon filled two water pails with the little silver fish.

I never expect to own a smelt tent. It is unlikely that I shall ever again go smelting. But I have the happy expectation of once again feasting on my favorite fish, smelts fried brown and crisp, and smelts-baked-in-a-beanpot.

berry picking

One of the pleasures of country living is berry picking. The lover of rural living needs no calendar to record the passing of the months. The reddening of the wild strawberries means the waning of June just as the coloring of the blueberries marks mid-July. The ripening of raspberries upon laden canes coincides with August's coming while the purpling of the blackberries is the harbinger of September. As each variety of berry has its own season, so the picking of each has its own distinctive appeal to the berrying enthusiast.

The gathering of wild strawberries is a leisurely task which is best undertaken in the afternoon when the sun has dried all the dampness in the field. It is well to go alone save perhaps for the companionship of an old dog who will not venture too far afield. There is always an element of surprise in searching for the berries in the meadow grass. Last May, for instance, the bank at the curve of the brook was white with blossoms and it was a disappointment later to find there only green leaves with one red leaf masquerading as a berry. There was compensation in finding a lush patch of berries in the orchard, a spot where berries had never before grown.

At best, the plots of berries are not close together and in seeking for the next spot there is the opportunity to look around. There is much to see and admire in a June meadow. Phoebes are building their nest under the old log bridge over the brook. A clump of jack-in-the-pulpit is thriving in the marsh at the edge of the field. Birds and flowers draw one away from berrying until the lengthening shadows warn the picker to return to her task. In no time the old white bowl is filled with fragrant berries and festooned with a clump of berries left on the stem. On the walk back to the house it is pleasant to contemplate the long summer ahead and to anticipate other berrying trips.

Leisureliness is usually lacking in the picking of blueberries. These berries grow in shadeless, burned-over fields where the rays of the July sun beat down so mercilessly that the picker hurries to fill her pail before the morning sun becomes too hot. One is glad to heed the bidding given at breakfast, "Come back with the berries in time for me to make a pie for dinner." It is pleasant to have company while one is blueberrying for the patches are so numerous and the bushes so laden with berries that two may pick side by side, chatting as their fingers fly. Even if a picker goes to the berry field without a companion, she does not find herself alone there. Song sparrows sing to announce that the field is part of their nesting area while chipmunks scold at the molestation of their domain. Long before dinner time a picker is glad to return to the kitchen with the announcement, "Plenty of blueberries this year for all the pies and muffins and preserves that you wish."

The gathering of raspberries deserves the designation of expedition. It is something not to be undertaken lightly or on the spur of the moment. Old clothes and sturdy shoes must be found. It is essential to secure the companionship of a neighbor because raspberrying holds hazards: the chance of going head over heels or the possibility of being lost in the raspberry patch, a slash-covered clearing of many acres. The family car must be borrowed for the trip because the clearings are usually several miles from the home place. The all day jaunt necessitates taking a lunch basket and thermos jug. Success in this venture calls for real strategy. It is necessary to select some landmark to point out the route back to the car; to locate a shady spot for the extra pails and the lunch; to stake out the best picking, which the experienced picker knows is beside a pile of rotting brush. There is little conversation as the pickers wade through the slash, for divided attention may result in upsetting the partially filled pick-dish or in shaking the unpicked berries from the canes. The pause for lunch is welcome. Completion of the day of picking is more welcome, for gathering raspberries is hard work. But it is rewarding work and the pails of red berries are tangible recompense for the long hours spent in the cut-down.

There is no compulsion associated with blackberrying. A few pies and a little jam is all the family desires. One goes to the blackberry patch from choice and not from need. The purple berries are numerous in the neighborhood but one chooses to walk to a patch near the shore where the salt air seems to make the berries grow large and flavorful. The pail is soon filled and there is time to walk along the shore. On the walk the picker reminisces about other berrying trips and regrets the swift passing of the summer.

Berry picking has a season of only twelve weeks but it is a task that gives lasting reward. All winter one can enjoy memories of the hours spent in a June meadow, the blueberry pasture, the raspberry clearing, and the blackberry thicket.

banking the garden

My garden is "put to bed for the winter." I use one of Grandmother Maddocks' expressions. I believe that the phrase is as apt now as it was half a century ago. Getting a flower garden ready for winter is a long process and it is one that I find enjoyable.

In August, I cut the seed pods from the perennials and pulled up the fading annuals. I always aim to pull up the encroaching weeds as well, but I never do.

This September I started a new practice. I pounded a stake into the ground beside the perennials, ignoring the phlox, the thistles, the astilbe, the lossestrife, and the asters. I often destroy a plant because of my zeal for early spring digging. This way I hope that my choice perennials will be protected. The marker stakes differ in color, length, and diameter. Not all were driven straight into the ground. I do not wonder that my callers smile at the sticks on crooked parade.

I gave the foxgloves special attention. A friend advised me that my foxgloves fail to winter over because I smother them with winter cover. I consulted an authority on gardens and he advised that each plant be covered with a wooden strawberry box weighed down by a rock. This was advice that I welcomed. I brought down from "up overhead" the frayed and faded baskets. I covered some thirty plants and topped each box with a rock brought from Schoodic. Now the parading sticks have colonies of pillboxes for neighbors. In deference to my friend, I covered a few of the foxglove plants lightly with leaves. I blanketed others with boughs of spruce. In the spring I shall be able to report which of the three winter coverings saved the most plants.

I regard planting as part of the chore of getting the garden ready for winter. Most of last year's bulbs succumbed to last winter's ice. This year I gave careful attention to the bulbs. I planted them where there is good drainage. I stamped down the soil above them. In December, I covered the bed with brush. The new choice lilies—Sun Ray, Ming Yellow and Hornbeck's Gold—have markers.

Dwayne, my garden helper, covered the rose circle. First, he surrounded the circle with a parapet of upended shingles. Then he covered the plants with dirt and hay. In early December, I banked the mound with boughs.

I have only two climbing roses of worth. These were covered in December. Around one I wrapped a pink coverlet of insulating material. Then I buttoned an old overcoat around it and forked hay over it. There was no insulating material for the second. I "made do" with an old sweater and hay. I covered both with boughs and bushes.

Recently I threw brush on the beds by the wall and the plank fence. Bruce had cut the brush in the pasture and along the margin of the meadow. I enjoy handling the boughs and breathing the fragance of the spruce. Only around the back porch did I press little firs and spruces into the ground. Last year I used many little trees around the sundial and along the driveway. By February the wind had blown many awry, giving the yard an uncared-for appearance.

Robert Frost wrote a poem about,

. . . saying good-bye on the edge of the dark
and the cold, to an orchard so young in the bark.

I do not say good-bye to my garden. I live beside it all winter. I do say the same things that Frost said of his orchard.

I don't want it girdled by rabbit and mouse,
I don't want it dreamily nibbled for browse
By deer, and I don't want it budded by grouse.

I say of my garden as Frost said of his orchard, no garden's

. . . the worse for the wintrest storm;
But one thing about it, it must't get warm.

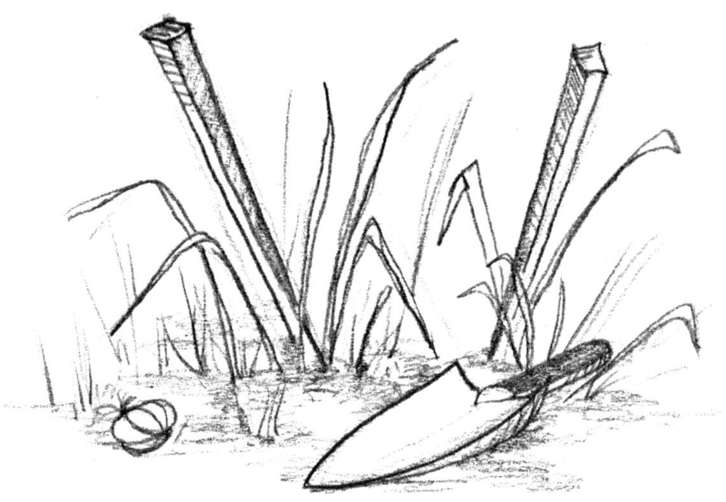

a pretty kettle of fish

"This is a pretty kettle of fish!"

For generations Maine men and women have been using this exclamation to express their dismay when things were not in a proper state of order and harmony. When Great-grandfather Friend used the expression—and he must have used it often because a saltwater farm in the early nineteenth century was not without its vexations—he likely thought of his great iron kettle, filled with boiling porgies.

Great-grandfather added to his meager farm income by turning fisherman and seashore manufacturer in midsummer. He built a weir across the home cove and in it he caught porgies. He took the red, oil-rich fish from the weir and poured them into a great kettle placed over a fire of dry wood on the beach. After the cooking the fish were pressed to remove the oil from the flesh, then the oil was stored in small casks. A Boston merchant came by schooner to pick up the oil that had been processed by Maine's farmer-fishermen. The fishing must have been pleasanter than the processing because the cooking porgies had a strong stench. The product was used in paints until it was displaced in the market by the less costly cottonseed oil.

The porgy kettle was retired from service about 1860. In my childhood it occupied a corner of Uncle's barn, where it became a repository for discarded meal bags, handleless hammer heads, teeth from broken rakes and varied discards of workbench and barn. When in time the kettle was filled, it well deserved the name given it by Aunt Nellie—"the clutter kettle."

My Grandmother Maddocks was a woman who was slow to express dismay or disgust. But now and then when she was sorely tried by some domestic crisis—quarts of cream that refused to turn into butter or a cake that unaccountably fell—she would cry in annoyance, "This is a pretty kettle of fish!"

I felt that I knew the kettle to which she referred. She had two iron kettles, each holding two gallons of liquid. She kept one for cooking meat and fowl: corned beef with its tasty accompaniment of vegetables, homecured ham, or a turkey to be parboiled before the roasting. The second utensil was the fish kettle. In it she cooked fish for the hens, not for the family. Every Thursday she bought a dozen fish heads from the fishman who peddled from door to door. Grandma cooked the heads in bubbling hot water. When I was very small, I liked to stand on a cricket and watch the bobbing heads in the kettle. After they were cooked, Grandmother pulled the kettle to the top of the stove tank and stirred meal into the mixture of fish and water.

In the late afternoon Grandfather took the food to the hen yard and I was his glad companion in dipping the mash into old tin pans and watching the hens gulp down the meal and, with cannibal-like glee, pick the flesh from the heads. When only the bones of the fish were left, my grandfather always made the same remark, "There is nothing as good as cods' heads to keep the biddies laying."

My mother, like her mother, used to now and then cry out in vexation, "This is a pretty kettle of fish!" When I heard her do so, I knew she was thinking of her chowder kettle, used to make steaming clam chowder. In it she tried out the pork scraps over a very hot fire and then she added a quart of water. Into it she dropped raw clams freshly shucked from their shells, cubes of potato, and slices of onions. When the ingredients were cooked she added salt and butter and two quarts of rich milk. After the butter was melted, she pulled the kettle to the back of the stove, where the chowder was allowed to "ripen" before it was reheated and served. The clam chowder made in the iron kettle, where hundreds of chowders had preceded it, had a flavor which defied description.

Farm economy and household custom have changed at Friend's Corner. Porgies have not been boiled for over a century. Great-grandfather's kettle now resides in the onetime tie-up where it holds peat moss.

No one at the Corner keeps hens and so, of course, no one cooks cods' heads for hens' food. Grandmother's kettle is upside down in the shed cupboard and has not been used for sixty years.

I make clam chowder (not as good as Mother's) in a stew pan of copper and steel, while Mother's discarded kettle sees summer service as a container for pink geraniums and ivy.

Though economy and custom have changed, our neighborhood vocabulary has remained the same. Last summer my neighbor Eva blew a fuse when she attempted to use her automatic washer and her electric frying pan at the same time. I knew just what she meant when she said, "This is a pretty kettle of fish!"

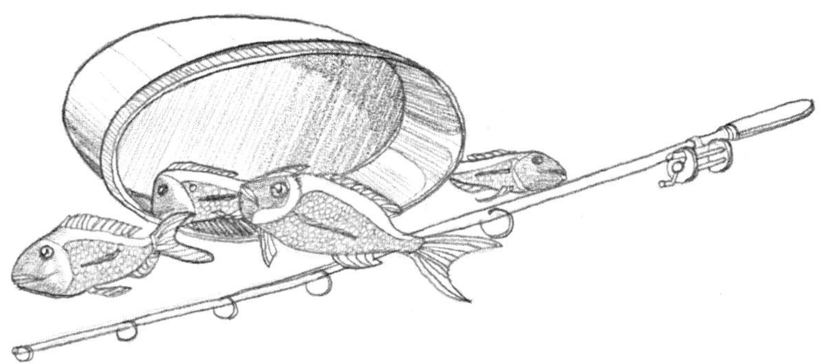

Country Foods

maine favorites

Maine natives have concern for good food. We insist that favorite foods be cooked the way our forebears cooked them. When a cook adds tomatoes, peas, and carrots to clam chowder, we regard it as contamination. We insist that blueberries are for muffins, pies, cakes, and puddings. We maintain that the berries have no place in ice cream and gelatin desserts. Homemade " 'east bread" is a Maine favorite. The sprinkling of caraway seeds or onion rings or chopped nuts on the tops of loaves we regard as near sacrilege.

Maine people are fish eaters. I believe that we eat some fish because of local loyalty, not because of the taste. Pickled herring and smoked alewives (pronounced "l-wives") are examples. The first were never served in our home. My friend Emily recalls that there was a crock of herring in the Clay cellar. When, on rare occasions, her mother cooked the fish for supper, she softened the culinary blow by making hot biscuits and topping the cake with extra-thick frosting. Every spring my father bought a string of smoked alewives from the store in Surry. The fish had been caught in Surry, smoked in Surry—I am sure that they were Surry's best. The string hung in the shed for days and scented the room with the odor of burning alders. At Father's urging, Mother finally steamed some of the fish. Father, loyal to the food of his childhood, used to exclaim, "These are every bit as good as those that Zenas Closson used to smoke." I noticed that my mother ate sparingly of the bone-filled fish and failed to speak words of commendation. When my father had forgotten about the alewives, Mother boiled the fish and fed them to the hens. Their odor lingered in the shed long after their bones had disappeared from the hen yard.

Today, people in Maine are less prejudiced about certain fish than they once were. Men and women of my parents' generation did not relish tuna fish. My father spoke for his contemporaries when he declared, "Never, never, will I eat horse mackerel." Like most Maine housewives of the early twentieth century, Mother had little use for cusk. When Father was going to the village and had been bid to buy a fish at the shop on the town wharf, Mother always gave the same directions, "Now John, don't buy cusk; it is not worth buying; it is not worth bringing home; it is not worth eating." Today, Maine natives eat both tuna and cusk and call them good. But two prejudices of our elders linger. Fried eels are not popular. I hear housekeepers say, "I can't abide the sight of eels. They look like snakes to me." Personally, I like eels. But I confess to an aversion to mussels. I have never eaten them and likely never shall.

Most Maine people have no liking for mushrooms. I have acquired a taste for them, but it took me decades to overcome the fear that the mushrooms in the casserole might be death-dealing toadstools. I have a Gorham friend who is a mushroom enthusiast. One day last summer he was driving along a back road beside a pasture. He stopped the car with a jerk; he could scarcely believe his eyes; the entire pasture was blanketed with tiny gray mushrooms, their undercaps faintly pink. He got out of the car and hunted up the owner of the pasture, who was shelling peas on the back porch. "Sir," he said, "would you mind if I picked some of the mushrooms in the pasture? I'd be glad to gather some for you." Replied the pea-sheller, "I don't mind. Pick them all, but pick none for me. I want to live many more years to feast on green peas." My friend went home for pails and baskets. His son and daughter returned with him. They harvested seventy quarts of mushrooms. Some they froze; some they put down in oil and vinegar; all winter long, they feasted on the "pasture fruit."

Maine people have decided views about baked beans. We hold

that beans should be baked long and slowly, preferably in an old pot; that salt pork, molasses (a big dollop of it), mustard, salt, and brown sugar should be companions in the pot. We maintain that ketchup, hot dogs and onions have no place in a Maine bean pot. We are particular about the dry beans used for the baking. We prefer Jacob's Cattle or Red Kidney or Soldier or Yellow Eyes. Pea beans are a second choice. No Maine man would choose to eat baked lima beans. The bread that is served with baked beans should be homemade yeast bread or brown bread or johnnycake. Muffins and biscuits are acceptable but never a first choice. Coffee cake and tea breads are totally unacceptable. Of course, homemade pickles must be the accompaniment of baked beans.

A Maine man has his garden favorites. He prefers Hubbard squash to the more recently developed varieties. He prefers spinach to endive and kale. He likes cabbage but not Brussels sprouts. He can arouse little enthusiasm for broccoli, less for eggplant. Peas, carrots, beans, corn, potatoes, and beets are his garden standbys. Tomatoes are raised for summer eating and autumn pickling. But the Maine gardener chooses to raise tomatoes that are large and round and red. He bypasses tomatoes that are unusual in shape or size or color.

A Maine native knows that in order to have good food, one must have good ingredients. A cook's attention is focused on five ingredients: molasses (does it have the proper flavor?), salt pork (is it fresh and lean?), milk (is it sweet and flavorful?), apples (are they tart and crisp?), potatoes (are they firm and mealy?).

Maine people show their concern for food by talking about it. Second only to the weather, food is their favorite topic of conversation.

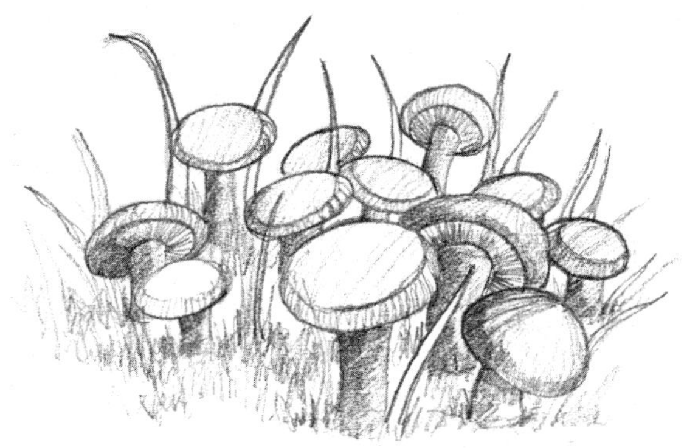

At the home place during the years of my childhood, we continued to use the recipes and the vocabulary of my seafaring grandfather.

Grandfather Wood gave up going to sea in the late 1870s. Attacks of malaria had weakened him; he had two young sons; his daughter, her husband, and four young sons lived in the neighborhood; his father-in-law, Grandsir Friend, was in failing health. So "Par Giles" decided to return to Friend's Corner to play the part of father, grandfather and head of the family.

When he sold his last schooner, the *Meridian*, he brought ashore numerous personal articles. He fastened his ship's bell outside the shed door and rang it to call his sons and his grandsons. He kept his spyglass behind the dining room door where he could reach it easily when a ship or a schooner appeared on the bay. He placed his 1854 compass on a high shelf out of reach of his youngest grandson. The dough table was moved from the schooner's galley to the farmhouse kitchen, where in turn Grandmother, Par Giles himself, and his daughter-in-law cooked for over half a century.

The Captain had started his seafaring career as a ship's cook. Flapjacks were his specialty. When his sons came home hungry in the evening, they did not hesitate to waken their father with the call, "Par Giles, please get up and fry us some flapjacks." The Captain would slip on his shoes, don an old reefer over his nightshirt and come to the kitchen to put an iron spider over the newly kindled fire. No one wrote down the rule for Grandfather's pancakes, but no doubt their special flavor and texture were derived from being fried in an iron spider greased with salt pork.

Father recalled that on occasion Par Giles made "folded jacks." These were spider-sized pancakes covered with applesauce, cooked cherries, prunes, jelly, or any other sweet found in the cupboard. The cooked and fruit covered flapjacks were then rolled. Grandmother felt that such use of sauce was wasteful and took to hiding the sauce. But her sons were good finders and sought out the sauce on the parlor whatnot, under the hall sofa, and in whatever unlikely place their mother hid the sweet.

When the Wood sons married, their wives were taught to make Grandfather's favorite desserts, his plum duff, and his Cuban cake.

Par Giles was a master hand at cooking clams and fish. Years later his sons sang the praises of his curried chicken, lamb stew, and cunner chowder, but, alas, no one had taken the pains to write down his rules. He continued to use numerous cooking terms that had been common aboard ship. He called a gingerbread "a Roger." He made his Roger with a mixture of hot coffee and hot chocolate. A combination of onions, potatoes, and fish cooked on the top of the stove had the unlikely name of "dog-on-the-shore." A dish made of clams baked between a layer of potatoes and a layer of onions was called "clams abed." Par Giles called meat hash "slumgullion" and he called fish hash "pothellion."

My father recalled that in his very early childhood, Elder Gilpatrick came in for supper one evening when the family was having the Captain's fish hash. Little John bowed his head for the blessing, but hardly had the Elder spoken "Amen" when the child shouted, "Good, pothellion for supper. I want a lot."

chowders, stews, and scouse

Maine people take a serious view of chowder. They insist that it be uncontaminated by tomatoes, peas, and beans. The thought of Manhattan clam chowder is revolting to a Down Easter. Tradition has it that a Maine legislator once introduced a bill into the legislature to make it illegal to add tomatoes to chowder within the State of Maine. The guilty party would be punished by having to dig a barrel of clams at high water.

The word chowder comes from the French word *chaudière*, meaning cauldron. Likely the word came to Maine from French Acadia, which was settled by Breton fishermen. In Maine parlance, a chowder is a combination of hot milk, potatoes, and onions with either fish or clams or corn. If potatoes are not added, the brew is called stew.

From a pre-1920 label for Blue Hill clams canned by the Sylvester Canning Company I copied a recipe for clam chowder. Those were the days when a clam digger did well to earn a dollar and a half a day.

Fry one-quarter pound of salt pork and cut in small pieces, add one quart of water, six potatoes and one onion sliced thin; cook twenty minutes. Then add one pound of clams, one quart of boiling milk, two finely powdered crackers and season to taste. Cook five minutes. Place in tureen six crackers, split in half, place butter the size of a walnut on each. Pour the hot chowder over these and serve.

Kind words should be written about potato chowder, sometimes called "scouse." Scouse is clam chowder without the clams. One of my friends who raised seven children praises the potato chowder: "We had a barrel of salt pork in the cellar as well as plenty of onions and potatoes. The cow gave us milk. Scouse was a popular supper dish with my children, especially if I made hot biscuits."

Chowder and stew are honored words in Maine. Bouillon is not highly regarded. Coastal slang goes like this, "Soupa de bool-yon, three buckets of water and one on-yon." A sailor once described bouillon as "so thin you can see bottom at forty fathoms."

In the last few years the word "stew" has taken on an aristocratic aura. This is due, I believe, to the popularity of lobster stew. The higher the price, the loftier the aura. Scallop stew, made in February of freshly dragged scallops is in my opinion the best of all stews.

Surely coot stew is the poorest. Fifty years ago I knew people living on Deer Isle who made coot stew. They insisted that it was good. No less a food authority than Kenneth Roberts wrote, "My grandmother was able to stew coot so that they were as delicious as black duck and as savory." A Brooksville friend tells me that coot must be soaked in saltwater overnight in order to be edible.

Fish chowder is a favorite with every coastal villager, but there is no agreement on what fish makes the best chowder. My mother chose cunners. So did Kenneth Roberts. Most cooks will select either cod or haddock. Dr. Philip Gray of Blue Hill, who makes fish chowder for lodge groups, prefers halibut. He feels that it has special flavor and richness. He removes the skin and the bones and places them in a cheesecloth bag that he puts in the chowder kettle. When he has a "chicken halibut" he also puts the head in the bag.

In the old granite company boardinghouse on Long Island Mrs. Lawson, a lady from Scotland, was the cook in the 1890s. She cooked for some two dozen boarders. She used two ten-pound haddocks for her chowders and she threw the heads of both fish into the broth. She brought the chowder in its big kettle direct from the stove to the dining table. Each boarder dipped out his own serving of chowder. Some were aghast when the ladle brought up a head with staring eyes. One man used to cry out, "Give me a harpoon and I'll spear the critter."

Maine people look askance at any changes in their favorite chowders and stews. One of my friends who is famous for his cooking of fish told me, "I often add garlic salt and curry powder to my chowders and stews but I do it *sub rosa*."

Maine people do not agree on what kind of crackers should be served with stews and chowders. Old-timers insist on round Boston crackers. Some support oyster crackers and some vote for cream lunch crackers or Pilot crackers. Saltines, with salt or saltless, also have their warm partisans.

We also disagree on what kind of pickles are best with chowders and stews. Sweet and sour, cucumber and tomato, chopped and ground—each has its supporter.

Down Easters may disagree on the best crackers and pickles but they are as one in agreement on the excellence of Maine chowders and stews—made, of course, with salt pork and uncontaminated by tomato.

baked beans and country suppers

"Please pass the beans" is the password at Down East country suppers. If the request is made of an out-of-stater, the reply is "Small, medium, or large?" If it is made of a native, he answers, "Pea, Cattle, or Kidney?"

There was a time when every Maine farmer raised his own beans. My friend Phyllis, brought up on a York County apple farm, recalls that her father raised three varieties: Jacob's Cattle, Yellow Eye, and Red Kidney. The beans were stored in small barrels in the attic above the woodshed. Phyllis was the youngest in a family of five children. It was her Friday afternoon task to fetch a quart of beans from the store room. She took a lard pail with her. In each barrel was a long handled dipper. Phyllis enjoyed stirring up the beans; she liked to hear them rattle. She looked for an occasional round rock or a dry bean leaf. She liked to fill the dipper with beans, hold it high above the barrel, tip it, and let the beans cascade into the barrel with a rush. She repeated a magic formula as the beans rattled into the barrel: "These are the Saco Falls, the Androscoggin Falls, the Niagara Falls." As her knowledge of geography expanded, she added, "These are the Yellowstone Falls, the Victoria Falls, the Zambezi Falls." Her play with the beans was always interrupted by a call from her sister, "Bring those beans right down stairs. Mama is waiting to put them in to soak."

Maine beans are put to soak Friday afternoon, parboiled on Saturday morning and bedded down in the pot with salt pork, molasses, salt, and mustard. The pot is filled with water, covered, then pushed into the oven. Maine cooks do not agree on the bean pot ingredients. Some omit mustard; some substitute brown sugar for molasses; some tuck a peeled onion into the pot. But they do agree on the cooking of the beans. They believe that beans are best baked in a woodstove; that the heat should never be higher than 350 degrees; that water should be added whenever the beans at the top are dry; that the cover should be removed for the last half-hour of baking. In the old days the baking period was from breakfast time to supper time.

Down East housewives prefer to bake beans in a used pot. The pot that Mother used was a secondhand one given her in 1896. It was still in use in the second decade of the twentieth century. Its handle was nicked, its sides were cracked; its cover was the top of a tin coffee can. Mother always washed the pot herself and she often remarked, "I wouldn't trust it in the hands of anyone else." Alas, one Monday morning the bean pot came apart in her hands. When Father came home from work she met him at the barn door with bad news, "The bean pot broke. It went all to pieces."

Father looked very sober indeed and he suggested, "Perhaps Nellie has an extra pot."

"No," said Mother, "I've asked her. "She has only one. Nor do Annie or Ethel have an extra one."

Father assured her that he would make inquiries among the workers at the granite yard. But every promising lead came to nothing. By Thursday it was evident that used bean pots were indeed in short supply. Father said, "Well since worse has come to worse, I'll buy you a new one at the Grange Store."

With unusual petulance Mother declared, "But I do not want a new one. I want an old one."

When Father came home from work on Friday, he was all smiles. Beside him on the buggy seat was a worn bean pot, nicked and cracked and coverless. When Mother saw it she exclaimed, "What a beauty! Wherever did you find it?"

Father replied, "I heard the rumor that Mrs. Warren Caly is going to Florida to live with Greeley. After work I went right to her house. She is going and she was glad to sell the pot. It was new when Greeley was a boy."

Mother used that pot for decades. It was among her most treasured possessions. My father made sure that there would never again be a bean pot crisis in his household. Whenever he heard of a sale of kitchen items at a farmhouse, he was there to buy the bean pot.

Beans at country suppers are often served with casseroles. Casseroles are good but they are poor substitutes for cold ham. Coleslaw and tossed salads also make their appearance with baked beans and they are tasty supplements to a country supper. But I miss the homemade cabbage salad and pickles our grandmothers used to donate to church suppers. One October, Mother counted the varieties of pickles at a Baptist supper. She noted the number in her diary: there were fourteen. I regret that she did not list the kinds. She did, however, write this comment, "Mrs. Wilfred Grindle's pickled quince were the most exotic."

Usually homemade bread is served with beans at a country supper. There is always a sigh of disappointment when a diner recognizes bakery bread. Most diners regard sliced yeast bread as a poor stand-in for hot homemade rolls, steaming and fragrant. Brown bread is now seldom used at a country supper. Few cooks steam brown bread, and it is difficult to keep warm. Perhaps people have lost their taste for this steamed wholewheat-cornmeal bread, rich and moist with molasses.

The return of woodstoves to Maine kitchens may mean that cooks will be baking more beans, and baking them as they should be baked. The household words at the Saturday night supper table may once again be, "Pass the beans, please."

hash for dinner

In east coastal Maine hash is a generic word. There is not one kind of hash; there are four kinds of hash.

Old-time sailor's hash is likely a thing of the past. It was made from meat, onions, and hard bread pounded together. Originally it was called "Lapp's Course" and then "lobscouse." My father's father was a sea captain. After he retired from the sea, he often made lobscouse for his two young sons. To the end of his days, Father called meat hash lobscouse. When he smelled hash cooking he would exclaim, "Good, lobscouse for supper."

He did well to exclaim "good," for Mother's hash was very good indeed. She used to remark, "There are three rules for the making of good hash." Her first rule was to use more meat than potato. She was careful to cut all fat, skin, and gristle from the meat. The second rule was to chop the meat and the potato separately. She chopped an onion with the potato before she combined the meat and the potato. One of our neighbors used to grind the hash ingredients. Mother's comment on the grinding process was, "Saves a lot of time but it makes a gaumy mess." The third rule was to fry the ingredients in an iron spider well greased with bacon fat or with pork scrap fat. Before the hash was fried it was moistened with cream or top milk. Meat hash should be cooked slowly, from twenty minutes to three quarters of an hour, depending upon the amount. When brought to the table, its top should be brown and slightly crisp, but inside it should be steaming and moist.

Red flannel hash is made from the leftovers of a boiled dinner. There are those who say that the hash is better than the dinner. Mother's rules for meat hash apply to red flannel hash. Again use more meat than vegetables; chop the meat and the vegetables separately; cook in an iron spider.

The rule for making red flannel hash may be always the same, but the ingredients may vary. Some cooks do not include onions with a boiled dinner; most exclude parsnips. It is safe to say that potato, turnips, beets and carrots are always part of the hash.

No combination of ingredients makes a more attractive hash than do the leftovers of a boiled dinner. Its brown crust is always deep in color; its edges show red. No hash is more delicious. The savor of the salt meat complements the flavor of the fall vegetables. My Great-aunt Fan always topped her platter of red flannel hash with half a dozen eggs, tenderly fried with their "sunny sides up."

Lovers of red flannel hash appear in every generation. My Uncle Arthur used to take it cold in his dinner pail for his noontime lunch at the Granite. My friend Phyllis maintains that red flannel hash sandwiches are her favorites. My godson, Nathan, likes to scrape the iron spider in which hash has been fried. He says of the scraps, "Better'n frosting."

In my childhood fish hash was a Sunday standby. It was prepared on Saturday. When the family returned from church and Sunday school hungry and tired, Mother fried the hash and dinner was soon on the table. Mother made the hash of any fish she might have on hand. Sometimes it was made from cunners and flounders that my cousins and I caught off the Slaven wharf. More often it was made from cod or haddock that Father bought on the town wharf at the village and brought home done up in newspapers. When Mother made fish cakes or hash for company, she insisted upon using halibut. She moistened the fish/onion/potato mixture with cream skimmed from the pans set in the cool cellar. I do not recall that she ever made hash from mackerel or from fish caught in fresh water. My father made it clear that he considered haddock and flounder and halibut vastly superior to trout and pickerel and salmon.

One of my friends who has been making hash for over seventy years tells me that she believes that corned fish makes the best hash. She prefers corned hake or corned pollack. She also likes hash made from soaked-out dried fish. I was surprised when she told me that she has made hash from trout and from salmon. Her comment was, "Hash made from fish caught in fresh water needs an extra lot of salt."

Generations of Maine people have been hash devotees. Maine cooks today make hash very much as their grandmothers did, but there have been changes in the foods served with hash. Our grandmothers always served hot bread with hash: corn bread—crisp and piping hot, or buttermilk biscuits—flaky and moist with shortening, or yeast rolls drawn freshly baked from the oven. The hot bread came to the table in a platter covered with a flannel tea cloth. Today's Maine cooks choose to place a loaf of French bread on the table. Each guest is invited to slice his own bread.

Pickles were once the concomitants of hash, and the pickles were not selected at random. Sharp mustard pickles and sour cucumbers were chosen to go with meat hash. Sweet pickles, either cucumber or pickled crab apples, were served with red flannel hash. Fish hash drew either dill pickles or bread and butter pickles. Today's cooks choose either to cook greens or to prepare a tossed salad for a hash dinner.

Food changes come and food changes go. Hash still holds its popularity in coastal Maine. I see no evidence that hash—meat, or red flannel, or fish—is about to follow lobscouse into culinary oblivion.

My Aunt Hannah used to remark, "I have molasses in my blood." That was her way of saying she liked to cook with molasses. It was her way of reminding her family that her father at one time earned his living in the molasses trade.

In the 1850s, and again after the Civil War, Grandfather Wood loaded his small schooner with Hancock County goods, bricks, shingles, and vegetables. He sailed to Portland where he sold the cargo. Then the schooner took on Saccarappa lumber, staves, and shooks that he carried to Cuba. On the return voyage the schooner brought molasses to Brown's sugar house on the Portland waterfront. The Captain always felt that he was a good judge of West Indies molasses. In later years Aunt Hannah set herself up as a judge of molasses, and she was a hard judge. Often I have heard her complain, "Do you call this molasses? I cannot taste any sweetness, only sulphur."

Many of the molasses dishes that Aunt Hannah used to bake are no longer made by Maine cooks. More is the pity!

Some twenty years ago a Congress Street restaurant in Portland had quite a reputation for its molasses apple pie. When a diner ordered the pie, the waitress raised the crust of a triangle of pie and doused the apple filling with molasses. Then she replaced the crust. The pie was good but it remained apple pie topped with molasses sauce. Real molasses apple pie has the molasses poured over the apples before baking. The molasses is cooked in the pie and becomes "apple of its apple."

Few people today bake molasses biscuits. But my friend Sylvia does, and she makes them for me once a year. She uses her regular baking powder recipe. After the biscuits are placed in a pan with high sides, she pours in the molasses, making sure that each biscuit is surrounded by the sweet liquid. In the process of baking, the dough absorbs some of the molasses. The rest of the liquid bubbles and hardens, making a caramel-like dressing for the bread. The biscuits are delicious and when one has them for supper, no dessert is needed.

Few people today fry apples. But my friend Mercy does, as did her Harpswell grandmother over a hundred years ago. She selects firm apples. Macs or Northern Spies are best. She pares each apple, cores it, and slices it. She takes care that the slices are thick enough so that they do not break. She fries the apple slices in an iron spider greased with bacon fat. When the apple slices are cooked, she shuts off the heat and pours in the molasses. The molasses bubbles and sizzles and browns the apples. Fried apples are ideal companions for pork and sausage and bacon.

All Maine cooks do make gingerbread. They do not make it as did my Grandmother Maddocks, who baked three kinds to please her molasses-loving husband. She made a hard kind that resembled thick cookies. It was so hard that the eater had to dip the gingerbread into tea or milk. She made muster gingerbread, a biscuitlike sweet. She used to say to me, "Your grandfather eats muster gingerbread from tradition, not from liking. It is the kind of gingerbread that his grandmother made for her sons when they went to Bucksport to drill in the militia."

Grandmother always laughed when her only son remarked, "You notice that two of the three sons went west in the 1840s. I figure that they went to escape the gingerbread." Grandfather did not laugh.

Every member of Grandmother's family ate the "spider gingerbread" that she cooked in her iron spider. It was rich with molasses, fragrant with spices, and moist with buttermilk.

I have done a little research on gingerbread recipes as they appear in recently published Maine cookbooks. All call for molasses, and I believe that the more molasses is used, the better will be the gingerbread. There is variety in the suggested liquids to be used: hot water, cold coffee, sweet milk, sour milk, buttermilk. Being Grandmother's granddaughter, I prefer buttermilk. I note with disapproval the tendency to dress up gingerbread with fancy names. I am not reconciled to the use of "sponge" or "bride's" or "light-as-feather" or "bird-on-the-wing" or "Jamaican" as adjectives to describe a sweet whose popularity is tested and accepted.

Molasses is of course a prime ingredient of molasses cookies. Again, I have done some research in Maine cookbooks. I am amazed at the great variety of molasses cookies, such varieties as I am sure Aunt Hannah and Grandmother never heard of. There are rolled cookies (some thick and some thin) and dropped cookies and bar cookies. There are cookies with raisins, with nuts, and with chocolate bits. There are cookies with fillings of dates or nuts or raisins or coconut.

Molasses is also a prime ingredient of brown bread, the steamed bread that goes so well with home cooked beans. Years ago Maine cooks stirred raisins into their brown bread. Once a Maine hostess was disturbed when she noticed that the new minister from Pennsylvania was not eating his brown bread. She asked, "Reverend, don't you like the brown bread? I notice that you are not eating it." Replied the minister, "Oh, you mean the fruitcake. I am saving it for dessert."

A further study of Maine cookbooks disclosed that the recipes for bran and whole wheat muffins call for the use of molasses, and that recipes for molasses doughnuts are included in all cookbooks. A very few give recipes for pulled molasses candy and even fewer give directions for making switchell, a haying-time drink that is made of vinegar, ginger, molasses, and cold spring water.

Today's Maine cooks may not have molasses in their veins but they do have molasses in their cookbooks.

People of Down East Maine take a proprietary attitude toward blueberries, that is, toward lowbush blueberries. They choose to ignore New Jersey blueberries; they regard highbush blueberries as being of inferior quality.

The home cook prefers that her blueberries be hand picked and she does not object to a few green berries in the box. Grandma used to say, "Sprinkle a few green ones on the top of the pie filling. They will add a sip of sour."

We Maine people are sensitive about what we consider the misuse of Maine berries. I was once served blueberry ice cream. The color was a dismal gray. I tasted the cream: the berries were frozen nuggets, the custard was of poor quality and strange flavor. No proper Maine cookbook contains a recipe for blueberry ice cream.

Nor should blueberries be combined with gelatin. Blueberries and gelatin are not kindred spirits. In a restaurant I was once served blueberry Jell-o. The berries, congealed in lemon Jell-o, looked for all the world like black shoe-buttons. They were as flavorful as shoe-buttons. Blueberries do not belong in frappés or souffles or cremes or compotes.

Blueberries belong in pies fashioned from home mixed and home rolled pastry, made with sugar, flour, and cinnamon, and baked in an oven with decreasing heat. Blueberry pie needs no trimming of whipped cream or ice cream. A slice of sharp cheese is appropriate, however.

Blueberries also belong in blueberry cake. There are two schools of practice in regard to blueberry cake. Some cooks mix the berries into a white cake flavored with cinnamon. Other mix them into a gingerbread batter. I belong to the second school and I prefer an all-molasses gingerbread. A topping of whipped cream or a glass of cold milk are equally good companions to blueberry cake.

Blueberries belong in muffins. They are at home in wheat muffins or oatmeal muffins. The secret of good muffins is using plenty of well-floured blueberries. The secret of superior muffins is using buttermilk or sour milk for the liquid. I sprinkle the tops of the muffins with cinnamon and brown sugar.

On cold, rainy mornings (and in Maine we have such mornings during the blueberry season) I serve stewed blueberries sweetened with brown sugar and flavored with cinnamon. I place a piece of buttered toast (homemade yeast bread is best) in the bottom of a soup dish and then fill the dish with the hot sauce. This is a breakfast to remember.

I notice that new cookbooks include recipes our grandmothers never knew: blueberry jam, blueberry pancakes; blueberry waffles; blueberry buckle; blueberry crisp; blueberry delight; blueberry tea cake. These recipes should be tried out and regarded as proper efforts to bring the berry up to date.

I notice that new cookbooks do not include the recipe for blueberry duff. This is a major omission. The duff should be made at least once in August and it had better be on a cool day. A biscuit-like dough is prepared and berries are stirred into it. The mixture is poured into a cloth bag. The pudding in the sealed bag is then boiled in water for about an hour. The glory of blueberry duff is the golden sauce that tops it. This is made by pouring a mixture of boiled water, sugar and flour into two beaten eggs. The sauce is flavored with lemon. Maine cooks maintain that blueberries have an affinity for both cinnamon and lemon.

Blueberries properly cooked are delicious. Certainly uncooked berries are just as delicious. A Maine man likes to eat the berries on his breakfast cereal. He likes to eat blueberries on lettuce for his dinner salad. He likes to eat blueberries and cream for his supper dessert. But best of all, he likes to eat a bowlful of berries and milk at bedtime. He takes his snack to the back step and eats in the dark. He gazes at the stars; he looks at the lightning bugs in the meadow; he listens to the loons on the shore. He is very apt to say to himself, "There is nothing as good as blueberries in August."

greening

In our country neighborhood the word *greening* had a seasonal meaning. In November and December it meant going to the woods to cut pine and hemlock boughs and to gather running cedar and princess pines. There were no conservation lists then and since the ground cedar and princess pines seemed to be more numerous every year, we did not hesitate to fill our bushel baskets with the fragrant greenery.

In May and June greening meant digging dandelion plants in the yard and in the saltwater meadows that sloped gently to the edge of the bay. Father frequently went with us on our winter greening jaunts but he was never with us when we went greening in May and June. He had more work to do in the spring months, and moreover, he refused to eat dandelion greens.

It is likely that Father's aversion to boiled greens was a reaction to his mother's fondness for them. He recalled that long before the dandelions were green, Grandma Wood served her family a concoction of fern tips, dock leaves, and purslane cooked with a piece of home-cured pork. Father used to declare, "It was a mercy that Mother did not poison the family."

My mother liked to eat greens and she also liked to cook them. She often said, "The steam from boiling greens and pork gives a spring smell every bit as good as the odor of lilacs." But she liked most to dig the greens. Sometimes she dug them in our yard, near enough for her to tend the fire and watch the oven. Other times she made an occasion of the greening and asked Cousin Ethel and Aunt Nellie to go with her to some neighborhood field where the dandelions came early.

Usually Olive, Alice and I were the greening companions of our elders, but we were not expected to dig. I am sure that the three women were pleased to be left to themselves to enjoy confidential talk not meant for little girls' ears. We kept in sight of the diggers but we followed our own pursuits. We threw rocks in the brook, we looked for sparrows' nests in the hardhack and we climbed the wild apple trees that edged the field.

When we returned to the house with our paper bags filled with greens, it was an evening's chore to cut off the dandelion roots, pick out the grass and weeds, and wash the plants. The next forenoon the greens were cooked with a junk of salt pork. Just before they were done, Mother dropped a half dozen peeled potatoes into the bubbling water, taking care to cook my father's potatoes in the oven. The boiled potatoes came from the cooking pot faintly green and flavored with an ambrosial combination of dandelions and pork.

When it came to dandelions, I was my mother's daughter. She and I always had two servings of the hot greens for dinner. At supper time we had them cold with slices of " 'east bread" spread with fresh butter. Our enjoyment of the greens was not spoiled by Father's comment, "I don't see how you can eat dandelion greens. I would prefer a serving of boiled running cedar and princess pines."

a salute to rhubarb

Spring in Maine means peeping frogs, forsythia, lilacs, and rhubarb. Writers in prose and poetry from Whitman to Jewett, from Hawthorne to Frost, have sung praises of the first three but been singularly silent about the fourth. I believe that rhubarb merits some literary recognition and in my humble way I propose to salute it.

In early spring the plants break through the ground in the form of red knobs that look for all the world like tight moss roses. After a few warm days each knob unfolds into long red stalks topped by great triangular leaves that suggest the parasol the tigers took from little black Sambo. What daffodils "casting their heads in stately dance" did for Wordsworth, a rhubarb patch does for me. On hot summer afternoons, on cold winter evenings, the patch flashes on "my inward eye."

It is pleasant to recall the rosy rhubarb knobs, the long red stalks and cool leaves. But it is more pleasant to recall the products of the patch: luscious pies, sweet tarts, and sauce with all the hues of a summer sunset. I make and eat sauce for weeks. Because I have never mastered the art of pastry making I have to depend on my friends for pies and tarts. When Margaret appears with a tart or Phyllis with a pie, my cries of pleasure fill the house.

My fondness for rhubarb goes back to my childhood, when rhubarb desserts were favorites in the three households that I knew best. Grandmother always made the first pie because Grandfather's patch was on a sunny knoll where the snow melted early. Grandmother made the pie the way Grandfather liked it. His mother had cooked for a family of eleven children and so from necessity had made pie in a long biscuit tin, covering it with a crisscross network of rich pastry. Though Grandmother's family was smaller, she also turned out biscuit-pan pies.

Great-aunt Fan cooked only for herself and Uncle Pearl and her guests. Her rhubarb pies were baked in brown earthenware plates that held a mixture of egg, rhubarb, and sugar. I especially remember the beaten egg because Grandmother, Mother, and Aunt Fan's four sisters made eggless rhubarb pies. Grandmother and Mother ate the Parker pies and made no comment, but not the four sisters. Maria and Mary, Georgia and Louise did not hesitate to speak their views about egg in the rhubarb pie: "Fan, egg and rhubarb do not combine well." "I cannot understand where you got the idea of pouring beaten egg into rhubarb pie. Our mother never did." "Cut me a very small piece of the pie, please." "No pie, please. I'll go to the pantry to see if there is a doughnut left over from breakfast."

Aunt Fan's defense of her pie was spirited: "Pearl and I like egg in rhubarb pie. The rule for it goes way back to colonial times when our ancestors, the Rideouts and the Bloods, came from New Hampshire to settle in Maine."

Every spring her four sisters visited Aunt Fan. She could have baked them a pineapple pie or a custard pie or a dried apple pie, but she always chose to bake a rhubarb. I liked to watch her make the pies. After she had arranged the rhubarb cubes in each pie shell, she added the sugar and poured in the beaten eggs, two eggs for each pie. She topped each pie with a circle of pastry in the center of which she cut a gigantic *E*. "There," she said as she slid the pie into the oven. "It is a matter of principle with me to put beaten egg in rhubarb pies. A woman should stand by her principles—especially when the principles were handed down from her ancestors."

I always ate Aunt Fan's pies but I preferred Mother's that were baked in glass plates, delicately colored with strawberry Jell-o, and eggless.

Today I eat Margaret's and Phyllis's rhubarb pastries with enjoyment and rejoicing. I rejoice also that the Durgins and the Lords handed down no culinary principles about the making of rhubarb pies.

dinner pails

A lot of good Maine food has been packed in tin dinner pails. Some sixty years ago the cutters and the quarrymen who worked in coastal Maine cutting sheds and quarries took their dinners to work in four-compartment pails. On the lid of each pail was a removable cup. Within the pail were two containers. The first, fitted into the top of the other container, was the pie saucer. The lower holder was designed to carry cookies, cake, and sandwiches. It fitted into the pail in such a way that there was a space under it for tea or coffee.

When a hungry man opened his pail he first found the pie, then the cookies and cake, next the sandwiches, and finally, the tea or coffee. One of Father's friends, Mr. Will Greene, a man of gentle manners and sweet tenor voice, had a peculiarity that amused his friends: he ate his way down through his pail. He ate his pie first and his sandwiches last.

Father ate his dinner in the traditional manner but his chief interest was on the pie saucer. He used to say, "Pie should be seasonal but apple pie is always in season." During the summer months he expected berry pies: strawberry and blueberry, raspberry and blackberry. Mother felt that the juice from berry pies was a hazard to the food in the lower compartment. She used to say to Father, "Take care not to tilt your pail. You don't want berry juice on your cookies and sandwiches."

He always made the same reply, "Who says I don't? Strawberry juice on a ham sandwich or raspberry juice with roast beef would be bully-good."

In the fall Mother baked squash and pumpkin and cranberry pies for my father's dinner pail. From Astrachan time to Northern Spy time she baked apple pies. When cold days came, she baked mince pies.

Father was very particular about the filling for the pies. He was so particular, in fact, that he was party to the making of the mincemeat. He insisted on using first quality apples, raisins, currants, and beef. He recommended that grape juice and strawberry preserves be stirred into the mixture as it cooked. Father had a low opinion of green tomato mincemeat. He would not knowingly eat it. At a Grange supper he was once served mock mince pie. He was a courteous man, and he ate it. When Mother explained that crackers were substituted for meat he was momentarily stunned but he managed to gasp, "Why, that is even worse than green tomato mincemeat."

In the deep of winter the granite yard closed so Father ate a hot meal at the family table. In March the yard reopened and Mother was again baking pies for the dinner pail. By March the best of the apples were gone; the cranberries and the squashes and the pumpkins had been used. So Mother baked pies with egg filling: custard, chocolate-custard, lemon, lemon-sponge, coconut, and caramel. Never did Father have the same kind of pie two days in a row. He knew he was fortunate. He used to lament over the fate of his friend Ward: "Ward's wife bakes a prune pie every week. A woman who does that is just about bereft of imagination."

Mother had plenty of imagination when it came to providing filling for Father's sandwiches. She used sliced chicken and beef and lamb and pork. She stirred up salad mixtures of chicken or salmon or eggs. She never used tuna fish. Too often she had heard Father declare, "Eat horse mackerel? Never!"

Sometimes she made sliced cheese sandwiches; sometimes she made a filling of cottage cheese and nuts. Often the sandwiches were supplemented with a crisp pickle or savory celery or a ripe tomato.

There were some foods that Mother considered inappropriate for inclusion in a dinner pail. She pronounced an indictment against each: "Frosted cake is too messy in the pail; doughnuts are too rich to eat with pie; breakfast biscuits harden in a pail; cream puffs get all over a man's hands and his clothing; a jelly-roll is sure to unroll; candy is meant for a between meal treat, not for dinner pail fare."

In the summer the granite cutters set their pails in the shade of the birches at the end of the cutting shed; in the winter, they set them in the corner of the blacksmith shop where the heat from the forge kept the food from freezing. Each pail had painted on it the initials of its owner. Sometimes Mother and Aunt Nellie arranged a surprise for Father and Uncle Arthur.The men were told to exchange their dinners. On that day Father ate from the *A.B.W.* pail, and Uncle Arthur ate from the *J.F.W.* pail.

The horses were fastened in a shed during the day. At noontime each owner gave his horse a bag of hay, a measure of grain, and a pail of water. Sometimes a horse was baited by the roadside. One morning when our Prince was given the privilege of grazing, he slipped his rope and enjoyed a few minutes of freedom. At once he went to the birches where the dinner pails were set, upset a pail and proceeded to eat the contents. When he was discovered, his nose was brown with peanut butter and a triangle of pie dangled from his mouth. That day Father gave his dinner to the man whose pail had been robbed and he shared his brother's dinner.

Saltwater
Seasons

early snowfall

When I was a child, I looked forward to the first snowfall. It often came during a night in late October, and when I awakened I found that the ground was covered with a sifting of white. I rushed out to write my name on the white coverlet of snow on the door rocks. If it were Saturday morning, my cousins joined me to play the game of "hound and hunted." The "hunted" hid in the pasture or the woods and the "hound" traced them by their prints in the light snow. The "hound" was always accompanied by Shep, whose excited barking added zest to the game.

Sometimes the snow was slow in coming. October and November would be snowless. By early December, when the trees were bare, the fields brown, and the roads frozen and rutted, people began to wish for snow to lighten the landscape and give sledding for the woodcutter. When the snow came at last, it was usually swept in by a northeaster that set the thermometer plummeting.

Once a surprise snowstorm came in mid-October when the colored leaves were still on the trees. When we walked to the district school at eight o'clock, we saw a bank of clouds to the east and

Cousin Austin said, "Maybe there will be a shower today." By the time of our 10:30 recess the air was filled with wet flakes falling rapidly. My Aunt Fannie, who was the mistress of the school, declared an indoor recess since we had come to school without our rubbers and jackets. Before the recess was over, Cousin Herbert opened the schoolhouse door and entered covered with snow. He was greeted with the cry, "Hello, Cousin Snowman." He ignored the greeting and announced, "I've come to tell all hands to stay here at noontime. The cooks of the neighborhood will send your dinners by way of Eskimo express and I'll be the Eskimo."

We were so excited over the prospect of having dinner in the schoolroom that for the remainder of the morning we had trouble keeping our minds on reading, history, and geography. As it was, Aunt Fannnie shortened the session when she heard Cousin Herbert call from the yard. He had brought our dinner on a "Cape Racer" covered with a piece of canvas from one of Grandfather's old sails. Evidently the mothers of the neighborhood had done some planning by way of the telephone. Harold's mother had sent a pan of biscuits, hot and buttered; Aunt Nellie had made a gallon of hot chocolate; Mother's contribution was hot vegetable soup; Ethel had made our favorite chocolate gingerbread. In a bushel basket our Eskimo had brought spoons, cups, and bowls.

Cousin Herbert accepted the teacher's invitation to have dinner with us. He and the teacher sat at her desk. Each child used his desk for a table. There was one topic of conversation—the snow. Wet and heavy, it was falling on the leaf-covered trees. The maples stood straight; the birches were bent.

When, at the start of the afternoon session, it was evident that we were too excited to do our usual work, my aunt announced, "This afternoon we shall have a special session in honor of the first snowfall. The older children are to use their dictionaries to find words associated with snow and storms. Write ten of the hardest on the board and we'll use them for our spelling lesson. Olive and Edwin are to search their readers and spellers for verses about snow. Select three, write them on the board, and we'll memorize them."

While the older children did their assigned tasks, we little children cut out snowflakes, using a pattern that our teacher had taken from the *Normal Instructor*.

The spelling list had been learned and recited, the verses committed to memory, and the blackboard decorated with paper snowflakes when Cousin Herbert once again appeared. This time the "Cape Racer" was loaded with coats and boots. It took us a few minutes to bundle ourselves up and to check on the fire in the stove. When we set out for home, Herbert made a path and we followed in single file. Because Alice was the youngest she was pulled on the sled and we laughed when we noticed that her scarf and mittens matched the red maple leaves on the big trees at the foot of Schoolhouse Hill.

The next morning the sun was shining. It was Saturday and we had the fun of making a family of snowmen—such a family as was never made before or since at Friend's Corner. Mother Snowman wore an apron of yellow maple leaves. Father Snowman had a scarf of crimson leaves and the snow children had caps of red sumac.

Every fall my father asked, "When will the first snow fly this year? Will there be an October sifting? Will the first flakes come in a November blizzard?"

My cousins and I always gave the same reply, "We hope that the first flakes will come with an October storm while the colored leaves are still on the maples."

sounds of winter

The jingling of bells was one of the winter sounds of my childhood. There was the tinkling of sleigh bells. The bells were attached to pieces of leather that were nailed to the thills of the sleigh. Sometimes each strap had as many as twelve bells, sometimes as few as four. Now and then the bells were fastened to a harnesslike circle that went around the body of the horse. Robert Frost's horse that questioned his driver's "stopping by the woods on a snowy evening" must have worn that circlet of bells. You recall the lines,

He gives his harness bells a shake
To ask if there is some mistake.

The bells varied in pitch. Some were loud; others were low. They varied in tone. Some were melodious; others were dissonant. The rhythm of the bells changed with the speed of the horse. We learned to recognize the sleigh bells of our neighbors, the village doctor, and the preacher who twice every Sunday drove by our house.

There was the dangling of the pung bells. Pungs were low slung conveyances on runners, long enough that a second seat could be added. A sleigh had style. A pung had none. It was built to take eggs and butter to the store and to bring back grain and groceries. Pung bells were larger and fewer than sleigh bells. They dingled and donged as the horse pulled the laden pung over snow-covered roads.

There was the clanging of sled bells. When men drove long, four-runnered sleds filled with wood along narrow, twisting woods roads, the sound of the bell warned other drivers of their approach. Each conveyance usually had one bell only unless the sled were drawn by two horses. The bell, large as a school bell, swung from a shaft of the sled. Sometimes it was attached to the harness hames and dangled from the horse's neck. Uncle Arthur's Dora refused to have a bell fastened to her but our black Prince enjoyed the bell. While he stood waiting for Father to finish loading the sled, he gave his head a shake that started the bell ringing. Father used to say, "Prince knows that this is the last load of the day. He is telling me that he is eager to get back to his hay and oats."

I miss the sound of bells, the tingling, the dingling, and the clanging.

There are sounds of the farmhouse kitchen which I no longer hear. On very cold nights Father "let the pump run down" lest the water in the pipes freeze. First he pumped water to fill the water pail. Then he held the handle high so that the water went out of the pump boxes down the pipe to the well. Strange sounds came from the pump: gurgling and glugging; dribbling and drippling. The next morning Father "caught the pump" by pouring water into the pump and jerking the pump handle up and down in short, quick jerks. Again there were unlovely sounds: first scraping and wheezing; then swishing and swashing; finally the splashing of water in the sink.

When Emily and I walked home from school on winter afternoons, we often stopped to listen. We heard the cold squeak of snow under our boots. We listened to the hum of the telephone wires. At the foot of the Sand Hill we caught the sound of cracking ice in Peter's Cove. On warm afternoons of late winter we paused to hear the babble of water in the roadside ditches and the plash of snow falling from the drift tops to the road. Often we heard the crows complaining about the ice-locked clam flats. We stopped to listen to the song of the chickadees and the notes of the nuthatches.

One afternoon we stopped so often that I was late in getting home. Mother was sitting by the kitchen window waiting for me. When she saw me, she threw her apron over her shoulders and hurried out to say, "I've been worried about you. What kept you?"

She knew what I meant when I answered, "The sounds of winter."

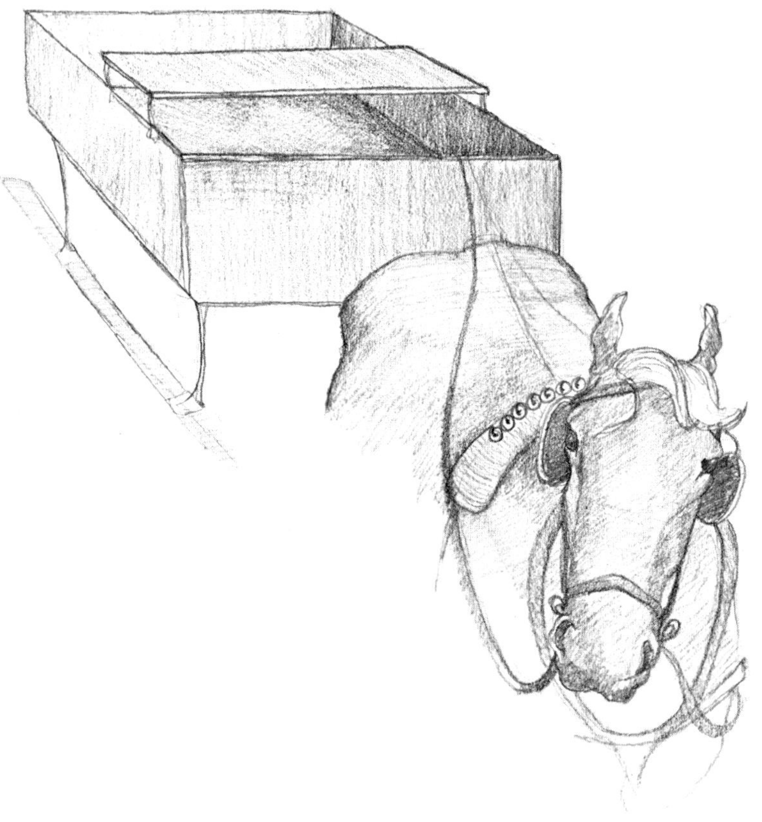

snowstorms

During a mid-January snow storm my young friends said to me, "What bad storms can you remember?" They were not amused when I said, "I don't remember the blizzard of 1888 or the gale of 1898." But all the same, I insisted upon telling them about those storms.

The great snowfall of 1888 was a late storm. It started on March 11th and in some areas of New England lasted through the 14th. It qualified as a blizzard: there was heavy drifting snow, the wind blew a gale, the thermometer went down to zero. Some areas received as much as forty or fifty inches of snow. New York City was hard hit by the storm. More than five hundred of its citizens were killed in the storm. One of the victims was Senator Roscoe Conkling, a Republican stalwart who was the foe of Maine's James G. Blaine. Blaine had dubbed Conkling "Turkey Gobbler."

The snow that came to New England the night of November 27th, 1898 is called the "*Portland* Storm" because the steamer *Portland* out of Boston, bound for Portland, was driven off her course and foundered off Cape Cod with a loss of one hundred ninety-one passengers and crew. Nearly thirty inches of snow fell. High winds did heavy damage both to ships at sea and homes ashore.

I hastened to tell my listeners that I recalled two great storms of this century: the December storm of 1962 and the Februrary snowfall of 1969.

The storm of 1962 followed the usual storm track up the Atlantic coast, but when it reached Yarmouth, Nova Scotia, it started a counterclockwise loop over central and southern Maine. In the course of its backward sweep it dropped forty inches of snow in a twenty-four hour period and brought sub-zero weather. For the first time in its one hundred twenty-eight years of operation, the *Bangor Daily News* did not go to press.

The February storm of 1969 gave one hundred hours of almost steady snowfall. Cape Anne got thirty-nine inches of new snow; Old Town, Maine, more than forty-three inches.

The January snowstorm of 1977 was followed by very cold weather. When my friends asked me, "Did you ever know a colder winter than this?" I was ready for them. "Yes, indeed," I said, "I knew the winter of 1917–1918." And I proceeded to tell them about it.

The winter of 1917–1918 saw the most extended cold wave recorded in New England weather books. For ten consecutive nights in late December and early January the temperature was below zero. Soldiers living in flimsy barracks were miserable; civilians suffered from a fuel shortage. Once, the thermometer at Van Buren, Maine registered forty-two degrees below zero.

I recalled that it was thirty-two degrees below zero at Friend's Corner. My father set up an old parlor stove upstairs. Both the inner and outer bay froze solid. Choppers on Long Island used horse drawn sleds to transport their cordwood to the mainland. Men raced sharp-shod horses on the inner bay.

Folks at Friend's Corner managed to keep warm during that winter. We were more than well fed. One of the culinary treats that Mother made for her family and the neighbors was what she called "frappé." She whipped a quart of cream, stirred in a cup of sugar and a cup of coffee. She poured the mixture into the White Mountain freezer container which Father buried in a snowdrift. In a few hours the dessert was frozen. Mother dipped it, smooth, sweet, and luscious, into her brown daisy-and-button sauce dishes.

My friends had looked gloomy as they listened to my weather

recollections but they brightened when I told them about the frappé. When I had finished speaking, one of them suggested, "Why don't we have some frozen cream? We've got the drifts; we've got the sub-zero weather!"

Spring Signs

A Downeaster smells spring before the calendar marks its official arrival. By mid-March the warm sun, an easterly blow, and a series of high tides have combined to free the coves and beaches of their covering of porous ice. The clam flats, exposed to the sun at low tide, give off an exhilarating reek, reminding a Maine man of the chowders and clambakes he has enjoyed through the years. The briny smell makes him think, too, of fish lines heavy with sea salt, and of August fogs loaded with moisture moving in from the Bay of Fundy. Despite the March wind and the biting air, he rejoices in the smell of spring.

On his own farm a country man will recognize other smells of spring. The rosette of red rhubarb leaves breaking through the ground has a tangy fragrance. The corner where the herbs grow—the box, sage, and southernwood—is a potpourri of smells. After the headiness of the herb corner, a man finds the orchard scents faint and hard to detect. The fruit trees bear hard, green buds, ready to burst after a few days of sunshine. When the farmer breaks open a bud he can smell the sap and he knows that his orchard will blossom and bear fruit. The stone wall beside the orchard is topped with rocks covered with lichens and mosses. He notes with surprise that they have started to grow and give forth a musty whiff.

But no spring odor pleases a Maine man more than the smell of his woodpile stacked foursquare against the side of the barn. With satisfaction he surveys it, estimating the cordage and congratulating himself on the quality of the wood. In the warm spring sunshine the odor of the February-cut wood is strong—the pitchy smell of pine and spruce, the pungency of cedar, the sweetness of maple, and the bitterness of birch.

On that warm day when a country man plows his land, he knows that ahead lies a season of hard but rewarding work. He takes pleasure in scooping up a handful of black soil and sniffing the earthy goodness. His animals graze in fields that will soon be lush and green. Nearby, in the middle of a plowed piece, is a brush pile topped with a dried Christmas tree and the fir boughs which banked the old house during the winter. The farmer smells their fragrance in the air.

But the smells are not the only signs of the change of season. The farmer sees a herald of spring in the haze on the hills and the pinkness of the buds on the swamp maples. He hears the notes of the song sparrows, the distant honking of the Canada geese winging northward, and the lonely call of the loons from the shore.

Later there will be more signs of spring. But March signs are enough to make a Downeaster declare, "I can smell spring today."

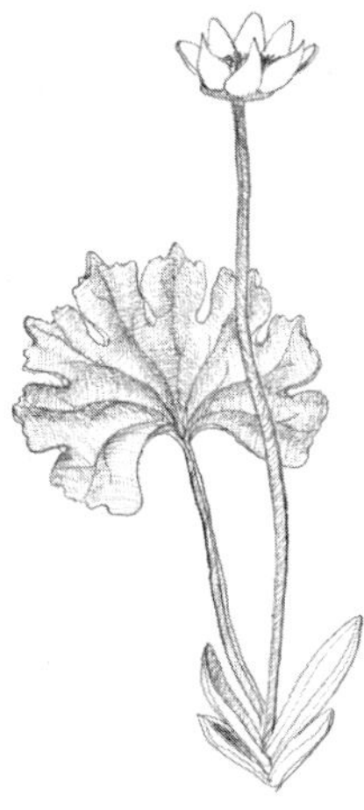

colors of spring

"Spring is yellow."

When I read this description of spring three weeks ago, I agreed. The pussy willow catkins had changed to fringed yellow flowers; the alders were hung with yellow catkins; the poplar leaves showed a yellow-green; the fly-honeysuckle on the hill was covered with small flowers that looked like pale yellow butterflies; the golden daffodils in the border were crowding the blue scilla.

"Spring is white."

Yesterday when I drove for the mail, I decided that spring is white. The stretch before Peter's Corner was veiled in white. Overnight the wild pear had blossomed. The five-petaled flowers are as white as tissue paper. Wild pear is the local name for this shrub that belongs to the rose family. Flower guides give other names; shadbush, Juneberry and sugar plum. It has two relatives that flower at the same time: the chokeberry, a low roadside shrub that the huckleberry and meadowsweet often hide; the tall chokecherry (in Maine called wild cherry). In late August all three produce berries on which robins, catbirds and waxwings feast. In my childhood the neighbors picked the wild pear berries for sauce and pies.

"Spring is green."

Today when I look at the pasture, the roadside, the fields and the lawn, I conclude that green is spring's color—not one shade of green but many shades. I have made the circuit of the house windows and counted the shades I saw. It numbered over twelve. I am not an artist and so cannot give a proper description of each shade. But I do recognize that Dodge's horse chestnut tree and O'Connor's willow are not the same shade of green; that the red leaves of the flowering crab contrast with the soft gray leaves of the apple trees; that the day lilies, the peonies and bleeding heart have foliage of varied shades of green.

As I write, I can see the large maple on my neighbor's lawn and the slender ones at the roadside margins. Next week they will come to flower. Then it will be time for me to change by description of spring.

"Spring is red."

wildflowers

The most common spring flower in the Friend's Corner neighborhood is the Canada mayflower, more appropriately called wild lily of the valley. The fragile starflower is second. Both are woodland plants that cover the ground with blankets of green. Bunchberries with tiny green flowers surrounded by large white bracts flourish in clearings and on highway margins. Violets grow in woods, swamps, fields, and pastures. Dwelley's *Wild Flowers of New England* states that five purple or blue varieties of violets are found in this region. Some spring I shall learn to identify each. Arbutus and bluets (Quaker ladies) are our first spring flowers.

I know where other spring wild flowers grow: wild oats (merry-bells), trillium, lady's slippers, gold thread, Clintonia (named by Thomas Jefferson for his political friend Governor Clinton of New York), lambkill, rhodora, pyrola, dewberry, self-heal and a dozen others.

Recently I saw a flower that I had not before found in this neighborhood though I had found it along the banks of the Saco River. It was alumroot, a member of the saxifrage family. The very small greenish flowers with orange tips are insignificant but the leaves are magnificent—three to four inches wide with seven to nine toothed lobes. They grow on long stems and have hair on the underside.

One day I left the road to follow a short trail, once the main highway. There I found a moosewood tree in full bloom. The flowers are a greenish white. I had to look sharp to see them under the young leaves.

I do not know the Latin names of the wild flowers. I enjoy the English names and take pleasure in turning the pages of my flower guides to look at the pictures and to read the descriptions. It is appropriate that many flower names are descriptive of the appearance of the plant or the blossom. A few examples are gold thread, bloodroot, Quaker lady, Queen Anne's lace, foam flower, twisted stalk, pussytoes, and butter and eggs. It is regrettable that some flowers have unattractive names: lousewort, cancer root, skunk cabbage, carrion flower, and feverwort, to name only a few.

Yesterday I had an adventure. In spite of the showers, Prim and I walked to the old paving wharf. Beside a brook near the wharf I found dogtooth violets growing, plants that I had not seen for half a century. Each plant has two long green leaves marked with purple spots; a single yellow flower grows on a long stem. Dwelley maintains that the flower is badly named. It is not a violet, and it takes great imagination to think that the leaf resembles a dog's tooth. The guidebook suggests, "Trout lily is perhaps the most fitting common name, because the plant is a lily and is often found flowering along brooks about the time when the trout season opens."

On some walk I hope to find wild columbines and flowering horseradish, plants that I have not seen for decades but which I knew in my childhood. Father used to pull the thick roots of the horseradish, wash them, grind them and then combine the pulp with vinegar and pepper to make a condiment to eat with Saturday's beans. If I find a wild columbine I shall leave it unpicked; it is too rare to break off and place in a vase. If I find the horseradish I shall leave it unpulled; the ground radish is too sharp for my taste.

deep summer

July is over and there are those who are glad. The week of searing heat pleased no one. Crops wilted; lawns browned; flowers faded; engines overheated and houses did not cool off at night. As one hot day followed another, people found it harder and harder to joke about the weather. Exclamations of, "It's an old scotcher," and "What a tan-toaster," changed to complaints of, "I never knew such a hot spell," and "This humidity is killing me."

The editor of the *Old Farmer's Almanac* reserved some of his most unattractive adjectives for the midsummer month of 1977. He described its weather as steamy, shinney, simmery, icky, and sticky. This year he must be praised for the accuracy of his prophecies. He foretold very hot weather for the period from July fourteenth to the twenty-first, with "brief relief" for the twenty-second and twenty-third.

Actually, few kind words are ever written about July. We associate the month with things we do not like: drought, heat, thunderstorms, sultry nights, forest fires, mad dogs, cicadas, ants in the pantry, crowded highways and violence in the streets.

July, however, deserves some commendation. In it are three significant anniversaries: that of the vote for national independence on July 2 1776; that of the Declaration on the fourth which justified the action of July second; the battle of Gettysburg on July first, second, and third of 1863, a Union victory that blasted Confederate hopes of English recognition and assured the eventual triumph of the Union.

In July, New England gardens yield their early harvest: tender lettuce, sweet green peas, beet and spinach and turnip greens. The parade of berries starts. The roadsides are still fresh and are starred with yarrow, Saint Johns-wort and wild roses. Vestiges of June remain: the ferns are still green; the birds continue to sing in the early morning; meadows are still lush.

July is the month when people enjoy the outdoors. Maine bays and coves are white with sails. People are tenting and camping. Fishermen go to the bay for mackerel and to the brooks for salmon and trout. July is "high tide" for the yacht clubs and golf clubs. Beaches and swimming pools draw children and teenagers. Gardeners tend their gardens; neighbors visit on front porches and decks.

July evenings at Friend's Corner have special attractions: the whistling of the loons at the shore; the glimmering of the Milky Way in the sky; the sparkling of the lightning bugs in the field; the keening of the nighthawks over the pasture.

July, I believe, deserves a better image than it has. Certainly it cannot compete in popularity with the holiday months of November and December. It will never have the appeal of May and April, the months of spring, or of June, the month of roses, or of September and October, the crisp months of goldenrod and purple asters. But certainly July has its special place in the progression of the months. Hal Borland described it best when he called it "concentrated summer."

the august garden

In late summer I had a letter from a friend who does not garden. She wrote, "Now that August is here I like to think of you sitting on the porch, admiring your garden and rejoicing that all the garden work is done."

It is true that I sit on the porch and admire the garden. But I work in the garden just as I did in April and May, in June and July; just as I shall in September and October. It is a gardener's joy that his gardening is never done.

The garden chores of August are varied. There is the labor of pulling up dead plants and erasing the traces of failure. This year I bought no petunias so I had no mildewing petunia plants to dispose of. Friend's Corner fogs do not provide a happy climate for petunias and sweet peas. But I did have sorry nasturtiums and ailing larkspur to remove from the beds.

There is another task that I call "barbering." I cut off the dead blossoms of the perennials so that the plants have a rounded contour. The poenies, the London pride, the moss roses, the astilbe and the pinks have been given their annual haircuts.

The day lilies blossom in August. Each blossom lasts only a day. I intend to cut off the wilted blossoms every morning. Dead flowers of geraniums and annuals need to be snipped off every morning to assure continued flowering.

I do not enjoy the August chores of staking plants. I never seem to have a stake of the proper height. The string breaks; I pound the stake into the ground at a crooked angle; I manage to tie the foliage either too tightly or too loosely. The sweet-scented geraniums under the parlor windows insist upon crawling in spite of all my efforts with stakes and cord.

In August I play the game of "floral chairs." I have a few extra plants that I move into the places where I have pulled up dead and ailing plants. Wax begonias, geraniums and marigolds transplant easily. I have some plants that this summer have grown happily in three locations.

The major task of late August is digging up the geraniums and setting in the mums for fall. This year the geraniums grew to an awkward size and faltered in flowering. This week I dug up sixteen plants from the beds in front of the porch and set them in wooden or pottery containers. I grouped them around the sundial and the white lilac. I am hopeful that the fresh soil and the new location will give them a second blooming spell. Then comes the delightful chore of digging deep holes for the mums and pouring water in the holes. I set the mums out according to color; the yellows, the rusts, and the deep reds. I was unable to buy white ones. I refuse to buy the rose ones. Neighbor Eva and I agree that pink has no place in a fall border.

August is the month to walk in the garden. I rejoice in my minor triumphs: the roses colorful with their third blooming, wax begonias making a pink and white blanket beside the blue ageratum, sweet-scented geraniums that are lush and green. The white phlox, the bee balm, the day lilies and the feverfew are always beautiful with little effort on my part. I lament my failures: the dead sweet Williams, the stunted Shasta daisies, the yellowed marguerites, and in a hanging pot the lantana that refuses to blossom. My failures never discourage me. They only prompt me to make high resolves for the next gardening season.

In a few days I shall write a letter to my friend. My reply will begin, "I am sorry that I did not write to you sooner. I have been kept from my desk by the urgency of my August garden chores."

news of the season

This is my letter to the world
That never wrote to me
The simple news that Nature
Tells with tender majesty.

Emily Dickenson

This is the season when Nature is telling us that summer is ending; that fall is coming. In mid-August the ferns hinted of the seasonal change. The sensitive ferns yellowed; the "cinnamon sticks" of the cinnamon ferns withered and dropped to the ground; the hay-scented ferns became as yellow as saffron. In September the interrupted ferns turned brown and the brakes changed from gold to brown to deep mahogany. Now, in late September, the royal ferns are still green.

Blueberry bushes also tell Nature's news. They change color in a dramatic way. First a few red leaves appear among the green, then suddenly the bushes are as red as though covered by a crimson blanket.

This week I took friends to Caterpillar Hill, red-hued with blueberry bushes. We came home by way of North Sedgwick where I had a happy adventure. Back of a white clapboard house that is being handsomely and properly restored, I saw a pumpkin patch. I stopped the car, got out and walked toward the house. Before I could knock on the door a fine looking young man rounded the corner of the house. "Good afternoon," I said, "May I buy a pumpkin?" The answer was, "Certainly not. It would be a pleasure for me to give you one." He picked up the largest of the three pumpkins under the dooryard maple tree and took it to the car for me. Now there is a great orange orb on my back step. It tells me that fall is here; that courtesy still flourishes.

September berries tell the news of the change of seasons. This year I have seen few bunchberries. Two friends who are interested in game birds have told me that the young partridges are especially numerous. No doubt the partridges and woodcocks have feasted on the bunchberries just as the robins are eating the berries of the mountain ash. The berries of the black alders are turning crimson. On the hawthorn bushes are berries still hidden by green leaves. The waxen bayberries were not allowed to ripen—the migrating warblers harvested them in early September. The purple claytonia berries growing by threes are my favorites. This year the birds ate them before I took the time to find and admire them.

In the fall I read the news that I have been a poor observer this summer. Always looking for wildflowers, I failed to notice the woodbine by the meadow brook. Now its red tendrils taunt me for my inattention. Nor did I notice the hawthorn thicket until the red berries appeared. The sweetbriar rose bush, relic of a long ago garden, went unnoticed this summer. Now its elongated tawny hips win attention.

Along the roadsides I notice the brown seedpods of wild perennials: the primroses, the daisies, the mullein, the thoroughwort, the cinquefoil and the meadow rue. The pods give promise that the roadsides will be seeded, and next summer the roadsides will be white and yellow with flowers.

Emily Dickinson wrote that Nature's news was told "with tender majesty." The adjective "tender" does not describe the majesty with which our New England maples declare the coming of autumn. They shout the news; they flaunt their colors; they wave banners. Nor does "modest" describe the asters and goldenrod that paint the fields and roadsides with purple and gold.

Nature speaks with many voices. Sometimes she sends her news in the gale and the hurricane. Then her majesty is awesome. Always in October she speaks in the forest. Then her majesty is beautiful.

In October, cold wind and a dusting of snow will bring the news that autumn is ending; that winter is coming. We must brace ourselves for the storms and the cold. Emily Dickinson commented on the coming of winter and gave a prayer,

Perhaps a squirrel may remain
My sentiments to share,
Grant me, O Lord, a sunny mind
Thy windy will to bear.

down east septembers

A country woman who for fifty years has watched the close of summer in the same Maine neighborhood should be an authority on Down East Septembers.

September once meant the opening of the district school. Children toting dinner pails filled with cold biscuits and cookies trudged the dusty road leading to the white clapboard schoolhouse that had been carefully cleaned by the neighborhood women in preparation for the first day of school. Today the district schoolhouses have become homes or shops or storehouses and the children are whisked by buses to consolidated schools where the cafeteria has displaced the tin pail.

The end of the summer was once punctuated by the country fair, an event that called for participation by every member of the family. Mother baked her whitest loaves of bread, grandmother brought out her most intricately designed quilts, and father harvested his largest pumpkins and squashes to bring to the fair. The children took a favorite pony or some sleek young creature for the livestock exhibit. The country fair still comes at the end of the summer but other attractions have long since displaced in importance the exhibition hall and the cattle shed.

September is still the month of blackberries in Maine and every rural woman aims to pick at least one bucket of the juice-filled berries. Picking blackberries is not a task to be undertaken lightly as is the gathering of wild strawberries and blueberries. When one seeks out strawberries in the June meadow, there is time to savor the fragrance of the timothy and to listen to the notes of the white-throat. Picking blueberries may well be a leisurely affair with time to admire the view and to seek out a sparrow's nest in the bushes.

When a picker is in a blackberry thicket, though, her attention must be centered on the briars and the berries. No flower and no fragrance should divert her attention from the briars that threaten her dress sleeves. No bird call and no bird's nest should make her fingers stray from the ripe berries that are ready, at the slightest swaying of the cane, to drop into the underbrush. A blackberry thicket abounds in underbrush, lurking roots, and hidden rocks. But the harvest is worth the hazards. Blackberries and cream, blackberry pie, and blackberry shortcake are favorites on every country table.

Maine roadsides in September look much as they did half a century ago though the roads are now blacktopped and the margins kept free of bushes. For three months the roadsides have been a green spread with touches here and there of white, rose, yellow, and purple from the shadbush, rose-of-Sharon, primroses, or fireweed, each blossoming in turn. At the end of the summer the greens give way to varied colors like those of a worn patchwork quilt. The beds of hay-scented ferns become yellow then turn to the tawny browns that match the darkening seeds of the fireweed. Rose-haws and bunchberries make dots of red against the tired green of shrub and plant foliage. Red horns of the sumac crown wayside bushes while chokecherries spill their purple clusters over gray cedar fence poles. The maples are still green in September but here and there an early turning branch makes a feather of red or yellow by the roadside.

The pasture brook now becomes a chain of shallow pools at whose muddy margins are the tracks of deer. Rocks worn smooth by the swift spring current are exposed, dry and bare. A country woman knows that a late September storm will restore the little brook and soon there will be a gurgling flow of water to make noisy waterfalls and to engulf the ferns and seedlings that in August took root along the brook's cracked edges.

September days usher in more than the usual "line gale" that fills the lagging brooks. Now and then they bring a hurricane. A Down Easter clocks the likelihood of the high winds by the old rhyme:

June, too soon
July, stand by
August, look you must
September, remember
October, all over

But September weather is made up of more than gales and hurricanes. The month has days as warm as those of July and others as cool as those of October, when the clear air seems to make the offshore islands miles nearer to the mainland. The noons are hot but at night there are hints of frost in the air and the careful gardener will by the last weeks of the month cover her tomatoes and zinnias with protecting newspapers.

It comforts a Maine country woman that through all the changes of half a century, some things have remained constant: the purple harvest of the blackberry thicket, the changing colors of the roadside, the fall fragrances of the rocky pasture, and the vagaries of September weather.